Standardized Testing
PRIMER

PETER LANG
New York • Washington, D.C./Baltimore • Bern
Frankfurt am Main • Berlin • Brussels • Vienna • Oxford

Richard P. Phelps

Standardized Testing
PRIMER

PETER LANG
New York • Washington, D.C./Baltimore • Bern
Frankfurt am Main • Berlin • Brussels • Vienna • Oxford

Library of Congress Cataloging-in-Publication Data

Phelps, Richard P.
Standardized testing primer / Richard P. Phelps.
p. cm. — (Peter Lang primers)
Includes bibliographical references.
1. Educational tests and measurements. 2. Ability—Testing.
3. Achievement tests. I. Title.
LB3051.P543   371.26′2—dc22   2007027972
ISBN 978-0-8204-9741-9

Bibliographic information published by **Die Deutsche Bibliothek**.
Die Deutsche Bibliothek lists this publication in the "Deutsche
Nationalbibliografie"; detailed bibliographic data is available
on the Internet at http://dnb.ddb.de/.

Cover design by Clear Point Designs

The paper in this book meets the guidelines for permanence and durability
of the Committee on Production Guidelines for Book Longevity
of the Council of Library Resources.

© 2007 Peter Lang Publishing, Inc., New York
29 Broadway, 18th floor, New York, NY 10006
www.peterlang.com

Printed in the United States of America

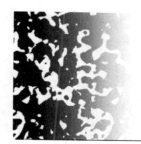

Contents

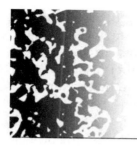

CHAPTER ONE

Introduction

Standardized testing bears the twin burden of controversy and complexity and is difficult for many to understand either dispassionately or technically. Moreover, there exist few media venues where a curious citizen can learn the topic either objectively or in depth. Journalists' coverage of the issue is woefully inadequate. Others who endeavor to inform the public can be profoundly self-interested or passionately ideological.

Nonetheless, standardized testing is a public issue and policy-makers and citizens the world over can and do make decisions affecting its character and use. It should be easier for them to understand the topic.

This is hardly the first primer on standardized testing, however. Previous ones, though, typically have been limited to two types. The first is produced by test developers or test sponsors and concentrates on reassuring consumers that a test is a valid, reliable, and reasonable instrument when employed for its intended purpose. These primers

can be short, even brochure-length, but the longer ones sometimes include sections on how to prepare for a test or interpret a test's results. Primers written by test developers sometimes suffer from a legally-careful timidity but are, nonetheless, usually instructive. A selected list of these primers is included in the appendix.

The second type of standardized testing primer is written by testing opponents. It may provide only that information, sometimes accurate and often not, that supports a certain agenda. Some of these primers resemble ideological or political manifestos.

One might identify a third type of primer, if one were to also consider testing and measurement textbooks. But, they are written for university students, typically at the graduate level, and assume a foundation of college-level statistics.

All previous standardized testing primers of which I am aware, however, tend to neglect most of the non-**psychometric** context of testing, such as: its effect on educational achievement; its extent of use and cost; the structure of testing systems; public opinion; relevant law and procedure; and test development methods. This one does not.

What is a "standardized test"?

A common misconception equates the term "standardized test" with those that use **multiple-choice items** and machine-readable (a.k.a., "bubble") answer sheets. To the contrary, if any aspect of a test—format, procedure, or administration—is standardized across test takers, it can be considered a **standardized test**. Thus, tests with written, oral, or otherwise "constructed" instructions or responses can be standardized, as can **performance-based tests** with skill demonstrations, exhibitions of work, structured real-time investigations, and oral interviews.

Physical tests, such as those conducted by scientists and engineers, also can be standardized of course, but here we focus on the measurement of

Latent trait

a trait that is not directly measurable or observable (e.g., knowledge, problem-solving skill, empathy).

Item prompt

the question, stimulus, or instruction that directs the test taker's response.

human **latent mental traits**. (Both surveys and tests measure mental traits. But, surveys typically measure attitudes or opinion, whereas tests typically measure proficiencies or aptitudes. Like surveys, however, tests are composed of items [e.g., questions, **prompts**].)

Educators and psychologists are the most frequent users of standardized mental tests. Educators measure academic achievement (i.e., mastery of knowledge or skills), diagnose learning problems or aptitudes, and select candidates for higher academic programs. Psychologists measure beliefs, attitudes, and preferences; diagnose psychological problems or strengths; and select candidates for employment.

Good standardized tests tend to be reliable—producing consistent results across time and conditions—and valid—measuring those traits that they are intended to measure.

The value and purpose of standardized testing

Standardized tests have a bad reputation in some quarters but, according to Professor Stephen G. Sireci (2005, 113), "it is an undeserved one." He continues

> People accuse standardized tests of being unfair, biased and discriminatory. Believe it or not, standardized tests are actually designed to promote test fairness. Standardized simply means that the test content is equivalent across administrations and that the conditions under which the test is administered are the same for all test takers. . . . Standardized tests are used to provide objective information. For example, employment tests are used to avoid unethical hiring practices (e.g., nepotism, ethnic discrimination, etc.). If an assessment system uses tests that are not standardized, the system is likely to be unfair to many candidates.

Standardized tests do not, and cannot, produce perfect measures, and no one claims that they can. But, other measures in common use are imperfect as well, some of them notoriously so. They include

some in medicine (e.g., cholesterol level, some cancer tests), meteorology (e.g., tornado prediction, hurricane tracking), economics (e.g., the multiplier effect, valuation), and in other fields where hard evidence measured with precision is highly valued, but not always obtainable.

The measures are used, despite their imperfections, because in most situations in science as well as in life some information for making decisions is better than none. Useful measures provide information whose benefits outweigh any cost and imprecision, and whose positive net benefits exceed those of any practical alternative. (Phelps 2000a, 2005a)

Standardized testing serves a variety of purposes. Some tests are designed to compare student scores to scores from a **representative sample** of students. Students are evaluated by how well they perform on the specified content (e.g., geometry) as compared to the representative sample. Standardized **norm-referenced tests** are an example of this kind of test, designed to measure a test-taker's traits relative to a norm group—typically a representative sample of peers from a large population of interest (e.g., all U.S. fourth-graders)—that typically covers a content domain determined by the test developer and not by a state or local agency or political process.

Other tests are designed to evaluate how well students demonstrate mastery of the specified content (e.g. algebra II). **Standards-based tests** are an example of this kind of test, an achievement test designed to cover a specified content domain that is usually identified by **content standards**.

Both kinds of tests provide information about the academic knowledge and skills of the students tested. The power of standardized testing lies in the fact that students take the test under similar conditions and that the tests are scored in a similar manner. Therefore, the student scores can be compared either to each other or to a threshold level of achievement. Arguably, the chief benefit of standardized testing is the standardization itself.

Representative sample

a sample is a subgroup of a population. A sample is representative if it accurately reflects the character of the population in the aspects under study.

Norm-referenced test (NRT)

designed to measure a test-taker's traits relative to a norm group.

Standards-based test

achievement test designed to cover a specified content domain that is usually identified by content standards.

Content standards

a predetermined, and sometimes legally-mandated, body of subject-matter content.

The demand for standardized testing

Not only are standardized tests useful, they are popular. The North American public has consistently favored the use of standardized educational testing, preferably with consequences (or "stakes") riding on the results, ever since the first polls were taken on the topic several decades ago. Depending on how the question is framed, those in favor of "high-stakes" standardized testing outnumber those opposed at ratios as high as twelve to one. Parents are stronger supporters of high-stakes testing than are non-parents, and that support does not budge when they consider the possibility of their own progeny failing.

A review of hundreds of opinion poll questions posed to education consumers—the public, parents, students, and employers—and to education producers—teachers, administrators, school board members—on the two most common types of high-stakes tests (Phelps 2005b, 14) reveals the following (see tables 1 and 2).

TABLE 1: SUMMARY OF PUBLIC OPINION ON HIGH-STAKES TESTING REQUIREMENTS AMONG EDUCATION CONSUMERS

Public support to require high-stakes tests for...	Number of polls	Mean percentage-point differential
...high school graduation	33	+47.3
...grade-level promotion	23	+45.3

SOURCE: multiple polls and surveys, U.S. and Canada, 1958–2003 (Phelps, 2005c)

Percentage-point differential is calculated by subtracting the percentage of negative responses from the percentage of positive responses and discarding neutral and non-committal responses. There are large positive differentials for either major type of high-stakes requirement—graduation or grade-level promotion tests. The positive differentials for

TABLE 2: SUMMARY OF PUBLIC OPINION ON HIGH-STAKES TESTING REQUIREMENTS AMONG EDUCATION PRODUCERS

Public support to require high-stakes tests for...	Number of polls	Mean percentage-point differential
...high school graduation	26	+34.3
...grade-level promotion	5	+38.4

SOURCE: multiple polls and surveys, U.S. and Canada, 1958–2003 (Phelps, 2005c)

Low stakes test

a test used to provide results that have only minor or indirect consequences for examinees, programs, or institutions involved in the testing.

low-stakes uses of educational standardized tests are even larger, with negative response proportions sometimes lower than five percent. (See Phelps 2005c)

Results from different polls approaching the topic in different ways suggest that most Americans would like to see high-stakes tests administered at least once at every grade level. Very few North American school systems offer this much standardized testing with high stakes for the students. With only a few exceptions, then, most North American educational testing programs fall short of what the public wants, and short of what most other industrialized countries have. (Note that the 2002 & 2007/2008 U.S. federal No Child Left Behind (NCLB) Act requires testing with consequences for schools, but not for students.)

Why is standardized testing, particularly when it has consequences, so popular? Because most

TABLE 3. RESPONSES TO QUESTIONS OF THE TYPE "HAS TEACHING OR INSTRUCTION IMPROVED BECAUSE OF THE STANDARDIZED TESTING PROGRAM?"

Respondent group	Number polls or surveys	Mean percentage-point differential
Education providers (e.g., teachers, administrators)	14	+39.6
Education consumers (e.g., students, parents, the public)	12	+50.8

SOURCE: multiple polls and surveys, U.S. and Canada, 1960–2003 (Phelps, 2005c)

Respondent group	Number of polls or surveys	Mean percentage-point differential
Education providers (e.g., teachers, administrators)	35	+36.2
Education consumers (e.g., students, parents, the public)	33	+43.5

TABLE 4: RESPONSES TO THE QUESTION OF THE TYPE "HAS LEARNING, EDUCATION, STUDENT EFFORT, OR STUDENT MOTIVATION IMPROVED BECAUSE OF THE STANDARDIZED TESTING PROGRAM?"

SOURCE: multiple polls and surveys, U.S. and Canada, 1960–2003 (Phelps, 2005c)

Teaching to the test

interpreted liberally, the phrase could refer to any instruction on subject matter that is covered by a test. But, teaching to the test is a genuine problem only when test security is lax and teachers have access to the exact or approximate content of an upcoming test. Otherwise, any teacher not teaching the same content domain from which a test has been developed is behaving irresponsibly.

believe, based on their own observations and experience (virtually all adults are veterans of over a decade of formal schooling), that it increases motivation and learning and improves instruction. This perception is verified in several dozen U.S. and Canadian polls and surveys conducted over the past several decades (Phelps, 2005c, 82–83), as shown in tables 3 and 4.

Indeed, questions of this type have never received a negative average response. Even studies negatively disposed toward standardized testing report that most respondents thought instruction had improved. Typically, the negative studies insist that instruction, improved or not, becomes encumbered by a "narrowed curriculum," **teaching to the test**, or similar alleged demons.

Organization and overview

The next chapter, chapter 2, distinguishes the two most basic types of standardized tests used in education—aptitude and achievement—by tracing their separate historical paths from their origins in the early nineteenth century to today. With this background, the most essential qualitative characteristics that make tests different, such as norms, criteria, standards, and stakes are described, along with the structures of educational testing programs and assessment systems. How tests are used, and which types of tests are used, varies from one country to

another; arguably, however, the testing regimes in North America have been the most atypical, though current trends suggest some international convergence.

Chapter 3 reveals the effects of standardized testing, both real and imagined, the responses that those effects have drawn, and the implications for testing system structure. The importance of these effects is illustrated in court decisions regulating test use and in debates among education researchers.

Chapter 4 focuses on the mechanics of test development, quality assurance, and program implementation that are generally manifest beyond the purview of all but the most knowledgeable and curious of the general public. Standardized tests are now developed through a demanding and time-consuming process according to detailed and rigorous technical standards that have, for many purposes, become legal requirements. Test development is organized according to one of two general frameworks—classical test theory or item response theory. Then, most standardized tests are administered in one of two formats—paper-and-pencil or computer.

Chapter 5 summarizes and integrates some of the previous chapters' main points and discusses their implications.

Finally, an ample list of helpful references and resources is included in the back.

GLOSSARY

Content standards—a predetermined, and sometimes legally-mandated, body of subject-matter content.

High stakes test—used to provide results that have important, direct consequences for examinees, programs, teachers, or institutions.

Item prompt—the question, stimulus, or instruction that directs the test taker's response.

Latent trait—a trait that is not directly measurable or observable (e.g., knowledge, problem-solving skill, empathy).

Low stakes test—a test used to provide results that have only minor or indirect consequences for examinees, programs, or institutions involved in the testing.

Multiple-choice item—a type of selected-response item that requires the test taker to select a correct response to a question (or, prompt) from among a small number of specific choices.

Norm-referenced test (NRT)—designed to measure a test-taker's traits relative to a norm group.

Performance-based test—requires the respondent to construct a response, demonstrate a skill, or follow a procedure. Examples include answering open-ended questions, conversing in a language, solving a mathematics problem while showing all calculations, writing an essay, or conducting a science experiment.

Psychometrics—the science of mental measurement. Experts in mental, or psychological, measurement are psychometricians.

Representative sample—a sample is a subgroup of a population. A sample is representative if it accurately reflects the character of the population in the aspects under study.

Standardized test—if any aspect of a test—format, procedures, or administration—is uniform across test takers, it can be considered a standardized test.

Standards-based test—achievement test designed to cover a specified content domain that is usually identified by content standards.

Teaching to the test—interpreted liberally, the phrase could refer to any instruction on subject matter that is covered by a test. But, teaching to the test is a genuine problem only when test security is lax and teachers have access to the exact or approximate content of an upcoming test. Otherwise, any teacher not teaching the same content domain from which a test has been developed is behaving irresponsibly.

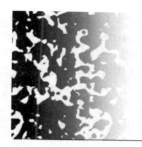

Aptitude or Achievement

Two Separate Historical Paths

Standardized tests have been with us for quite a while. Some cite the millennia-old Chinese civil service examinations as the oldest-known large-scale written standardized tests (Zeng, 1999, 8). Such would be fitting in one sense—apparently, the ancient Chinese tests were intended to be both **summative**—measuring specifically how much applicants had already achieved (i.e., how much they knew)—and predictive—estimating how much they might achieve in the future, by measuring the breadth of their knowledge and skills, even testing their skill at poetry. The tests were, at once, both achievement and aptitude tests. (DuBois 1964)

Generally, **achievement tests** are designed to measure how much you have learned in the past. Achievement tests cover subject-matter content and are meant to measure the level of knowledge or skill attained within a content domain. Most teacher-made classroom tests are educational achievement tests. (a.k.a. proficiency test).

Summative assessment

when achievement tests are used to summarize the accumulation of knowledge up to that point.

Achievement test

designed to measure what has been learned, rather than to predict future performance.

Aptitude test

designed to predict how much you might learn in the future.

Aptitude tests are designed to predict how much you might learn in the future. They do this by testing content-free mental abilities or measuring as wide an array of knowledge and skill as they can, with no particular attention paid to what one "was supposed to" have learned in the past. They assume that those who have the widest base of knowledge and the best developed set of information processing skills can most easily build new knowledge later.

But, the scientific study and development of standardized testing as we know it today began much more recently, in the 19th century, in the slipstream of the advances in mathematics and statistics in the preceding centuries.

Origins of educational achievement testing

In the United States, the origins of standardized educational achievement testing are often attributed to the work of Horace Mann in the mid-1800s and of Joseph Mayer Rice at the *fin de siècle.* Their motives for standardizing education quality measurement seem to have been similar, but their methods and goals appear to have been quite different, as were the types of achievement tests they developed.

Horace Mann ranks among the most influential figures in the history of American education. He promoted structuring schools into grade levels, classes, and courses; limiting public finance to secular schools; formal training for teachers in teachers' colleges (i.e., normal schools); the founding of the first state normal school in the United States (in Lexington, Massachusetts); and compulsory attendance laws, both to assimilate immigrants and to pull more citizens into the civil society. Mann also advocated state, rather than local, control of the public schools, and served as Secretary of the Massachusetts Board of Education from 1837 to 1848. (Butts, 1947; Lincoln & Workman, 1936; Kaestle, 1990)

His "friend and fellow-reformer," Samuel Gridley Howe was, like Mann, an admirer of the centralized Prussian school system, bureaucratic hierarchy,

defined structure, graded classes, and well-articulated curricula. When elected to the Boston school committee in 1844, he realized that a central authority needed an information feedback mechanism with the individual schools if it was to efficiently manage them. So, he set about to "revolutionize the collection of data on the performance of children in the grammar schools." Along with colleagues, he "devised uniform written tests for the top class in each of the grammar schools—a single standard by which to judge and compare the output of each school, 'positive information, in black and white,' to replace the intuitive and often superficial written evaluations of oral examinations." (Tyack, 1974, 35).

Mann and Howe introduced standardized tests in the Boston schools to gain "objective information about the quality of teaching and learning in urban schools, monitor the quality of instruction, and compare schools and teachers within each school" (Gallagher, 2003, 85).

Mann and Howe's standardized written tests were of the type still most widely used today throughout the world. They were not "scientifically" developed but, rather, larger-scale, standardized versions of tests that any individual teacher might develop. They were meant to be standards-based tests—with test content based entirely on the subject-matter content of classroom instruction—the curriculum—or, more precisely, the **intended curriculum**. One of their motivations for testing was to gauge whether the intended and the **enacted curriculum** were the same in all schools and classrooms. If a test revealed, for example, that fourth-grade students in some classrooms did not understand certain mathematical concepts they were supposed to understand at the same time their counterparts in others classrooms did, it might indicate lapse or misunderstanding on the part of certain teachers.

Boston's program of standardized written tests became so popular it was adopted by school systems across the country, including in New York State,

---

Intended curriculum

the subject matter content that is planned for school instruction, according to legislated and/or published standards.

Enacted curriculum

the subject matter content that actually is taught in the schools regardless of original intentions.

where the Regents examinations were first administered in 1865. The first Regents exams were high school admission tests, with minimum scores required for students to receive state tuition aid. The tests proved so popular, though, that New York's colleges soon pressed the state to develop a similar program for them. Eventually, Regents examinations were introduced in all high school subjects, providing "uniform and dependable measures of pupil achievement, year by year"(Tinkelman, 1965).

By the mid-twentieth century, Regents high school achievement tests were offered three times a year in 25 different subjects. They varied in comprehensiveness, however, with some covering the work of a single year and others multiple years.

Regents tests were **criterion-referenced**—each student's performance was judged in comparison to certain expected levels of mastery. Thus, the number and proportion of students who passed any given Regents test could vary substantially from year to year. (The alternative to criterion referencing is norm referencing, where student performance is judged by comparison to other students'; norm-referencing is common with institutions selecting from a candidate pool for a fixed number of places (e.g., university admissions, employment hiring, military recruitment.)

Mann and Howe used standardized tests primarily for two purposes, the first of which was system-wide quality control. Their tests were management tools and monitoring devices, though individual schools could use them for their own purposes. Arguably, the purest descendent of this type is today's system monitoring test, the most prominent of which is the National Assessment of Educational Progress (NAEP), administered from the 1970s on.

Mann and Howe's second testing purpose was to maintain content and **performance standards**—a sentiment very familiar to us today. Their tests were standards-based tests, as are virtually all contemporary high-stakes education tests, whether administered in North America or elsewhere.

Criterion-referenced test (CRT)

a test that allows its users to interpret scores in relationship to a functional performance level, for example, the degree of competence attained by a particular student, without reference to the performance of others.

Performance standards

specify the level or levels of achievement expected.

One might say that Mann and Howe were men of their times in one respect—in advocating the creation of an American meritocracy or "hierarchical social structure organized by ability" (de Marrais & LeCompte, 1999, 10) and ahead of their time in another—in advocating a more "scientific" management of American schools.

Living half a century later, Joseph Mayer Rice shared the latter interest. Rice is regarded by some as the inventor of the scientific standardized test. But, whereas Mann and Howe used tests primarily as management tools, Rice used them for basic research. Mann and Howe wished to know if curricula were being taught; Rice wished to know if curricula should be taught. (Engelhart & Thomas, 1966)

Rice trained to be a medical doctor, specializing in pediatrics, and practiced for a time in New York City. He became interested in the fledgling sciences of psychology and pedagogy at some point and traveled to Germany, his parents' homeland, to study with some of their originators and to observe European school systems. (Houston, 1965)

Upon his return to the United States, he became an outspoken critic of American schools and their instructional methods. In tune with political moods and movements at the turn of the century, he wrote a series of muckraking magazine essays about the alleged poor state of American education, and a string of books, including *The Public-School System of the United States* (1893), *The Rational Spelling Book* (1898), and *Scientific Management in Education* (1913). In the process, it is said that he traveled the country, observing hundreds of classrooms and speaking with thousands of teachers, administrators, board members, and parents. (Butts, 1947; Lincoln & Workman, 1936; Rodgers, 1984)

He reported that most U.S. classrooms relied on tedious instruction and unsuccessful, rote learning. Like Horace Mann before him, he thought that schools could be organized more rationally and that instruction and learning could be analyzed scientifically. Much like his scientific management contemporary, Frederick W. Taylor, of time-and-motion-study

fame, Rice wished to make the tedious and mundane parts of the learning and instruction process more efficient, to free up time for higher and better uses.

In the pursuit of this interest, he developed spelling tests to measure the details of the process, and gave them to teachers to administer. The results of these non-standardized test administrations, however, were too erratic to be meaningful. When he tried again, the forms and procedures were standardized (he conducted most of the test administrations himself) across over 30,000 individual test administrations. Moreover, he recorded background variables for each test taker, such as age, nationality, environment, and type of school.

Rice's study was an early version of a multivariate statistical analysis, and his spelling survey represented an early version of an individual **diagnostic test**, hundreds of which are in use today.

Some educators and psychologists of his era criticized Rice for "trying to measure things which by their very nature could not be measured." (Lincoln & Workman, 3) But, only several years later, E. L. Thorndike conducted similar studies of handwriting and went a step further, developing perhaps the first scientifically constructed psychological measurement scales (that converted **raw test scores** to **scale scores**), and grounding psychological measurement in the methods of statistical science.

Diagnostic test

its purpose is to ascertain, prior to instruction, a student's abilities and level of achievement so that instruction might be adjusted appropriately.

Raw score

the unadjusted score on a test, perhaps the simple number of correct responses, with no accounting for variations in item difficulty or weighting.

Scale score

the result of the mapping of a raw test score onto a more meaningful, interpretable, or comparable scale.

Origins of educational aptitude testing

The first practical application of methods to measure human mental abilities, it is widely believed, began in the late 1800s, most prominently with the studies of French physiologists Alfred Binet and Théophile Simon. Their immediate objective was to devise tests for identifying children with mental deficiencies who might require special attention.

Binet and Simon assumed that the mind comprised separate, and separately-measurable, functions, such as association, attention, memory, motor skill, reasoning, and will. So, they developed a test

Norms

the results of a test administered to a "norm group"—a representative sample of a larger population of interest.

Age-equivalent score

the chronological age in a defined population for which a given score is the median (middle) score.

Mental age

a unit for expressing the results of intelligence tests based on comparing the individual's performance on the test with the average performance of individuals in a specific chronological age group.

Intelligence Quotient (IQ)

a unit for expressing the results of an intelligence test, based on the ratio of an individual's mental age (MA), as determined by the test, to their chronological age (CA): IQ = MA/CA x 100.

Intelligence test

test designed to measure an individual's level of cognitive functioning not related to any particular subject matter.

Mean

the arithmetic average of a set of scores (i.e. the sum of a set of scores divided by their number).

for each separate function and classified test items within each by level of difficulty (i.e., they *scaled* them). A series of carefully-selected questions tested children's common sense, judgment, and mental speed and agility.

Binet and Simon experimented with a variety of measures and combinations before settling on the scale that would endure. Giving the same test to large numbers of children enabled them to establish **norms** for each chronological age (i.e., **age-equivalent scores**). Children whose **mental age**, as measured by the Binet-Simon test, fell far below the norm for their chronological age were identified as retarded. Eventually, the **intelligence quotient** would be calculated by dividing the mental by the chronological age (and multiplying by 100). (Gottfredson, 2007)

The Binet-Simon test was revised for the American culture and population at Stanford University and remains one of the most widely used **intelligence tests**. The Stanford-Binet, a direct descendent of the original, consists of over a dozen subtests, including: vocabulary, pattern analysis, comprehension, copying, number series, memory for digits, memory for sentences, equation building, and paper folding and cutting. Its scale is set with a **mean** of 100 and a **standard deviation** of 16. Thus, an IQ score of 132 falls in the upper five percent of the distribution of scores, and a score of 68 in the lower five percent. One of the most common uses for today's Stanford-Binet remains the identification of children who might require special attention. (Brubacher, 1966)

In 1911, H. H. Goddard brought Binet's model to the United States. For Goddard, "[The] mission was to convince public school officials to incorporate student intelligence testing into their decision-making processes." (Gallagher, 86) Indeed, some of the early intelligence tests were used, appropriately or not, for individual psychological and education diagnosis. But, one of their most popular uses then—for educational program placement decisions—remains popular today, most commonly as one of several

Standard deviation

the square root of the average squared deviation around the mean (i.e., the variance). It is used as a measure of variability in a distribution of scores.

Aptitude

potential for future learning.

pieces of evidence used in placement decisions for gifted and talented and special education programs.

With the United States' belated entrance into World War I, the army required a method for quickly identifying potential officers among the large numbers of recruits. Robert Yerkes, a primatologist and president of the American Psychological Association, and Arthur Otis formed a committee of experts to develop a screening device. Their first product was the Army Alpha Test, a group-administered, paper-and-pencil, multiple-choice instrument intended to gauge a recruit's mental capacity—his **aptitude**. Some attribute the origins of academic tracking and ability grouping to the aptitude testing of this era. (see, for example, Gallagher, 88) But, the practices of tracking or grouping students (by perceived ability) goes back at least as far as Plato. (Brubacher, 1966, 162) Moreover, as mentioned earlier, they were already a popular school management and structuring device in the mid-1800s, and they grew even more fashionable due to the Progressive Era's fascination with scientific education. It is true, however, that after they became widely available, aptitude tests were often used for student placement in tracking and grouping schemes.

The most famous use for aptitude testing, however, would be in university admissions. According to Zwick (2007), in the early twentieth century, university applicants

> . . . faced with a bewildering array of entrance examinations that differed widely across schools. In an attempt to impose order on this chaos, the leaders of 12 top northeastern universities formed a new organization, the College Entrance Examination Board, in 1900. The College Board created a set of examinations that were administered by the member institutions and then shipped back to the Board for hand scoring.

The first College Board examination comprised achievement tests in nine subject areas. The *aptitude* test—the Scholastic Aptitude Test—came decades later, with test items similar to those that had been

included in the Army Alpha Test. The machine-scored, all-multiple-choice format came still later, in time for World War II and the deluge of G.I. Bill college applicants immediately after.

In more recent decades, the SAT has eschewed most of its aptitude character in favor of more **achievement** characteristics, even reducing its name to include only its original acronym, SAT. Its rival, the ACT (formerly, American College Test), was from its origin a curricular-based achievement test. Every few years, ACT conducts its National Curriculum Survey of educators and derives the content of the ACT assessment from those results.

Achievement (or, educational achievement)

the accumulated knowledge and skills acquired from previous learning.

The gloom of the past

Many observers choose to trace the origins of standardized testing in North America to the early aptitude tests. For critics, this allows them to associate current testing with long-dead racists of the early days of intelligence testing when many considered eugenics a credible scientific pursuit. They can retell the sordid tales of yesteryear in order to shame today's tests by association.

In retrospect, the assumptions of some of the earliest developers and users of aptitude tests were naïve and, certainly, some of their practical applications were improper and even bigoted. But, they were a century ago. Besides, all of today's sciences have embarrassing forbearers. The first astronomers, physicists, and chemists were astrologers, wizards, and alchemists. All the sciences have learned from the mistakes, naïveté, and misuse of their early years and matured to make enormously beneficial contributions to the well-being of humankind. The sciences have grown up, as have each of us.

Today's psychologists know far more about their instruments and their application than did their earliest predecessors, benefiting from over a century's worth of learning and the accumulated wisdom of tens of thousands of researchers and research studies. Some consider standardized testing to be the greatest single social contribution of psychologi-

cal science (Gottfredson, 2007; communication with Roediger, December, 2006).

In their zeal to chain today's standardized tests to the ignominy of aptitude testing's troubled adolescence, however, critics ignore most of standardized testing's long and rich history of achievement testing. Even in the alleged glory days (or, perhaps, inglorious days) of intelligence testing—the first few decades of the twentieth century—standardized achievement testing was far more common. The era's few and limited uses of intelligence tests are much written about today, whereas the era's popular and numerous standardized achievement tests are assumed to not have existed. According to Monroe (1950, 1461), in the decade between the years 1917 and 1928, 1,300 different achievement tests were developed in the United States and, by 1940, there were twice as many, dwarfing the number of different aptitude and intelligence tests in use.

Lohman (1997, 88) attributes the popularity of school testing in the early 20th century to "an educational system overrun with pupils." Citing Tyack (1974, 183), he reported "From 1890 to 1918 the population of the United States increased 68%. High school attendance . . . increased 711%. On average, more than one new high school was built every day during this period."

According to Lincoln and Workman (1936, 4, 7), writing about the same historical period, " . . . the use of standard tests was accelerated by the discovery that the marks and ratings given by teachers cannot be relied upon as being accurate. Many investigations have given evidence of this fact."

According to Butts (1947, 605), "The testing and measurement movement had a great rage in the 1920's and 1930's as a means of making education scientific. . . . The testing movement was applied to nearly all the school subjects in the form of achievement tests and was perhaps the most characteristic feature of scientific educational procedure in the 1920's."

According to Holmen and Docter (1972, 34), "the first successful commercial test publication in

the United States was done by the World Book Company which published the Courtis Standard Research Test in arithmetic in 1914." In 1930, the Cooperative Test Service of the American Council on Education began to administer achievement tests at schools and colleges, ultimately on 650 different topics (Butts, 1947). Six years later, the Educational Records Bureau began using the first test scoring machine, the IBM 805, to expedite the grading of standardized tests administered on a large scale by the Cooperative Test Service.

University admissions testing in the United States

Prior to World War II, the College Board's mission was simple and straightforward. But, its work agenda expanded dramatically during the war years. In addition to testing applicants for admission to selective colleges, the College Board was drafted to develop and administer **selection** tests for the U. S. State Department and the military branches.

Selection

choosing individuals based, in whole or in part, on their test score (e.g., for university admission, a scholarship, employment).

In 1947, in part to unburden itself of much of the detail and technical work, the College Board joined with the American Council on Education and the Carnegie Foundation for the Advancement of Teaching to create the Educational Testing Service (ETS). Each of the founding members would unload the responsibility for the continuing development and administration of one or more testing programs onto ETS. The Carnegie Foundation contributed the Graduate Records Examination (GRE) and the Pre-Engineering Inventory. The American Council on Education added the National Teacher Examinations and the Cooperative Test Service, while The College Board turned over the Scholastic Aptitude Test, as well as the Law School Admission Test (LSAT) and several other programs.

The SAT today is owned by the College Board and developed and administered by ETS. Its only real competitor emerged in 1959 as the American College Testing Program. Now known simply as ACT, it has differentiated itself from its rival in two aspects. First, it has always been an achievement test, with

its content derived from the National Curriculum Survey it administers to teachers and other content experts every few years, whereas the SAT was a curriculum-free aptitude test for many years and, some would argue, has not yet managed a complete transformation to an achievement test.

Second, the ACT was born in the era when the SAT was still meant for, and essentially managed by, a consortium of selective, private colleges; the ACT marketed itself as the college admission test for everyone else and, even today, the country's heartland is also its own. (ACT 2007a)

At this point, virtually all U.S. postsecondary institutions accept either the ACT or the SAT with an enrollment application. When someone says that a particular U.S. state is an "ACT state" or an "SAT state," they refer to the state's public universities' dominant preference, typically bred through familiarity. Historically, the SAT has been preferred by the states lining the east and west coasts (plus Indiana and Texas), whereas the ACT has been preferred by all the other states that lay between the Appalachian and Sierra Nevada ranges. More applicants take the SAT, but more state systems seem to prefer the ACT.

U.S. federal testing programs

With the passage during Lyndon Johnson's presidency of the Elementary and Secondary Education Act (ESEA) of 1965, the federal government issued its first educational testing mandate. Title I of the ESEA provided federal funds for school districts with a sufficient proportion of poor students, as "compensation" for their educational disadvantages. In return for Compensatory Education funds, however, districts were required to administer pre- and post-tests to Title I-funded classrooms. They used national norm-referenced tests (NRTs) purchased from commercial vendors, administered the tests themselves, and reported the results to the federal government.

Despite the prevailing public perception, the No Child Left Behind (NCLB) Act of 2002 did not start a new federal testing program from scratch. With federal education acts coming up for renewal every several years, the NCLB Act itself was, administratively, simply the 2002 version of ESEA renewal. The testing requirement remains part of the act's compensatory education section, Title I. The federal government's leverage remains the funding it provides for compensatory education programs.

The NCLB Act differs from previous incarnations of ESEA in that it requires testing of all students in several grade levels, rather than just those in schools with high proportions of poor children, and it promises stiffer consequences for failure to achieve average test scores above a certain threshold. Also, with NCLB, all tests should be based on state standards. Whereas, previously, schools used norm-referenced tests for Title I testing, under NCLB they use criterion-referenced tests.

The other federal testing program is the National Assessment of Educational Progress (NAEP), created by the U. S. Congress in 1969. The NAEP is an achievement test, to be sure, but is based not on any particular state or local curriculum, but a generalized one. From its origins, the NAEP was designed to be a monitoring test—providing a "snapshot" of U.S. education—based on complex samples of voluntary tested classrooms with equally complex samples of test items. The NAEP bears no stakes for individual students, teachers, or schools. Indeed, the identity of individual test-taking students is not recorded.

The NAEP is overseen by a bi-partisan governing board (the National Assessment Governing Board [NAGB]) and sponsored by the U.S. Department of Education. Periodically, NAEP has gathered educational achievement data from 9-, 13-, and 17-year-old students, or from those in grades 4, 8, and 12 and occasionally young adults, in one or more of ten subject areas. Different subject areas are periodically reassessed in order to record possible changes in education achievement, with the content statistically equated from year to year to aggregate trends.

Before 1990, NAEP scores were reported for the nation as a whole. Beginning in 1990 with one grade level of mathematics, the NAEP has been administered to representative samples in every state choosing to participate. For all but the largest states, participation in State NAEP required an agreement to supplement the national sample with more participating schools.

In 2002, the NCLB Act made participation in the State NAEP mandatory, so that its test scores could be used as benchmarks against which to compare trends in scores on state tests.

Federal educational testing programs other than Title I and NAEP have been proposed. President George H. W. Bush's initiative, America 2000, included an outline for American Achievement Tests. They were to comprise voluntary national examinations in five core subjects at grades four, eight, and twelve. The proposal was taken very seriously and much preparation work was completed, but the plan died when President Bush failed to win re-election.

President Clinton proposed federal support to develop and administer annual Voluntary National Tests (VNTs) in reading at the fourth-grade level, with content and structure derived from the NAEP Reading test, and mathematics at the eighth-grade level, with content and structure based on the Third International Mathematics and Science Study (TIMSS) eighth-grade mathematics test. The tests were intended to set benchmarks to help states and local districts focus their programs and the measurement of their students' performance. The President offered to provide full federal funding for the first year's administration and all funding for start-up and ongoing test development. The VNT legislation, tabled during President Clinton's second term, did not make it out of the U.S. Congress.

Moreover, several federal agencies other than the Department of Education have long been involved in test development. For example, the Department of State has had its foreign-service exam

and the U.S. Civil Service Commission its selection tests.

The Armed Services Vocational Aptitude Battery (ASVAB) is one of the most widely used large-scale aptitude tests, as the U.S. military not only administers it to its own recruits, it offers it free of charge to any U.S. high school. The ASVAB contains eight sections: general science; arithmetic reasoning; word knowledge; paragraph comprehension; mathematics knowledge; electronics information; auto and shop information; and mechanical comprehension.

Stakes

For understandable reasons, standardized tests tend to attract more scrutiny when they bear consequences, or *stakes*. Fail an occupational licensure examination, for example, and one may receive no license despite having successfully completed a substantial amount of coursework. Fail a secondary school graduation test, and one may receive no diploma, despite having spent over a decade in school.

Moreover, when tests have consequences, they can attract a good deal of criticism, especially from inside the education profession, and from journalists (Phelps, 2003).

Declines in average college entrance examination scores in the 1970s and poor U.S. showings on international examinations in math and science gave rise to a fear that education quality was deteriorating. In an effort to reverse the perceived decline, reforms of the 1970s and early 1980s emphasized returning to basics and establishing minimum performance standards.

Minimum competency tests were established in most states and their passage required for graduation from secondary school. Most of them were administered as **power tests**, not **speeded tests**. Eventually, enthusiasm for them dimmed, however, when some observed minimum competency tests motivating low achieving students but driving down standards and expectations for other students.

Minimum competency test

a high-stakes test that requires performance at or above a single threshold test score before certain educational attainment will be recognized.

Power test

test administered with no effective time limit.

Speeded test

test administered within a time limit such that some test takers may not finish.

Moreover, some states were using commercial tests based on national norms and not necessarily tied to the curricula faced by their students. Indeed, many states had no state curricula or content or student performance standards, making it difficult to argue in court that students throughout a state had been exposed to the content on which their minimum competency test was based.

In 1989, representatives of the U.S. federal government met with the nation's governors and agreed to cooperate in education policy efforts. The Charlottesville, Virginia "education summit" established six national education goals—Goals 2000—and formed the National Education Goals Panel. In 1994, the U.S. Congress added two more goals. The goals were aspirations and benchmarks rather than requirements, were not met in the year 2000, and have since been abandoned.

One practical result of that era of state-federal cooperation, however, was funding for efforts to write national standards for most subjects, starting with the National Council of Teachers of Mathematics' (NCTM) effort. Non-binding national standards were written for most subjects in the 1990s, and generated intense ideological battles that continue unabated (e.g., between "traditionalists" and "constructivists," between the "child-centered" and the "teacher-centered")

Early in 1996, forty-three of the nation's governors met in a second "education summit" in Palisades, New York, along with corporate chief executives from their states and other invited guests. The second summit's governors agreed to develop and establish within two years internationally competitive standards and **assessments** to measure progress toward meeting them. The standards writing efforts continued, and more states adopted high-stakes, standards-based testing programs.

Ironically, some of the loudest complaints about the NCLB testing requirement concerned the stakes. Many seemed not to realize that NCLB required no stakes for students (ergo, they may not even have tried to do well on the tests). The stakes held for

Assessment

generally refers to large-scale, systemwide measurement programs for pupil diagnosis, program evaluation, accountability, resource allocation, or teacher evaluation.

schools that could get shuttered and, indirectly, for teachers who could lose their jobs if their school closed or enough of their students transferred to others.

This asymmetrical arrangement, with high stakes for schools and teachers and no stakes for students, would likely seem strange, or even demeaning, to teachers from the rest of the world where such arrangements scarcely exist. In most of the world, students bear the consequences for their own test performance and, generally, schools and teachers do not.

North American exceptionalism

Ironically, aptitude tests, which were first developed in Europe, became popular for use as large-scale education tests only in North America. By contrast, achievement tests, first developed scientifically for use on a large-scale in North America, were relied on almost exclusively outside North America for large-scale assessment. Only in recent years have large-scale aptitude tests gained some popularity outside North America, and then primarily as system monitoring and diagnostic tests.

Systemwide test

any test that is administered to all students or to a representative sample of all students within a jurisdiction for at least one grade level.

In most of the world, the content of **systemwide education examinations** has always been common standards and curricula. Teachers align their instruction and students their study, to them. Most of these tests have consequences and, typically, are placed at the entry and/or exit points of levels of education (e.g., as **end-of-level tests**). Most countries require both upper secondary exit and university entrance examinations as well as either lower secondary exit or upper secondary entrance exams.

End-of-level test

test administered at the end of an educational level, such as primary or secondary.

In their eight-country study of secondary school examinations, in a chapter titled "Lessons for the United States," Eckstein and Noah (1993, 238–239) wrote:

> In addition to certification and selection, other countries use their end-of-secondary-school examinations for a variety of other functions: for example, to define what knowledge and skills are of most worth, to set performance expectations of

students, teachers, and schools, and to provide yardsticks against which individual schools and the school system as a whole can be assessed.

The United States . . . lacks any systematic and general way of certifying completion of a specified course of secondary school study and, unlike other countries, has no consistent national criteria or means for selection beyond that stage, whether for employment or for particular types of postsecondary education or training.

In the United States and Canada, however, where education governance is more fragmented, common standards and curricula have been difficult to implement and enforce. In the place of standards-based (i.e., criterion-referenced tests) tests, many U.S. states and school districts purchased norm-referenced tests from commercial test publishers. The norms were constructed through field tests with national samples of students on a generalized curriculum of their own construction. In the absence of standards-based testing, aptitude tests were often used to make highly consequential decisions, such as retaining students in grades, awarding students scholarships, or admitting students to selective schools or universities.

Other standardized testing features that have been more common in North America than elsewhere on the planet include: machine scoring, selected-response and multiple-choice item formats, commercial test development firms operating in competitive markets, and standardized university admission tests.

Typically, outside North America, by contrast,

- consequential large-scale standardized educational achievement examinations have been developed, essentially, as extra-large versions of classroom tests, with open-ended questions written and scored by groups of classroom teachers.
- educational tests have been developed, administered, and scored by governmental agencies.
- universities have administered their own entrance examinations.

Likewise, the politics of standardized testing differs between North America and the larger world. Much of North America's political rhetoric and journalistic coverage remains existential: . . . are standardized tests good or bad? . . . should we use standardized tests or not? For North American test developers weary of these debating points, political discussions in some other countries, where journalists and the general public alike accept tests as givens and discuss, often with considerable expertise, the quality or appropriateness of test content in some detail, might seem refreshing.

State math or American math?

Frustrations with education reform efforts often energize appeals for high-stakes national standards and national tests in the United States and even, occasionally, in Canada. Some of the appeals are naïve—of the "all we need is the political will" type. Unfortunately for national test advocates, it would require much more than will.

Like it or not, the U.S. Constitution says nothing about education. Therefore, the nation's original founding entities—the states—are responsible (by deference) for it. We can have national tests in the U.S., but they cannot be standards-based, criterion-referenced tests without an amendment to the federal constitution, or the legislative equivalent. Like it or not, one can have West Virginia reading and West Virginia math, but there is no such thing as American reading or American math. States set standards, the United States does not. A state can have uniform curricula, the U.S. cannot. And, like it or not, state standards and state curricula vary substantially. (see, for example, American Federation of Teachers, 2006; Shaw, 2007)

A couple of years ago, I tried my hand at writing mathematics test items. I gathered all the textbooks available to me and noticed (1) they teach a lot in the schools now that they did not teach when I was a kid (e.g., proofs in elementary school, discrete math (i.e., networking, graph theory, etc.), explor-

atory data analysis in elementary school, stats and probability in middle school) and (2) no two textbooks are alike. If one added up all the content in all the, say, 4th-grade textbooks, one would end up with 3 three years' worth of math instruction. No single school can teach all of it. Topics, and the sequencing of topics, vary from state to state and district to district. To expect students who have studied exploratory data analysis and graph theory to do just as well on a test that covers those two topics as they might on a different test that covers different topics (to which they have not been exposed) is unreasonable.

Granted, some of the professions, after decades of negotiation and struggle, have gotten all, or almost all, of the state legislatures and occupational licensing regulators to allow them to use a single examination nationwide (though, in some cases, the states still set the passing score). But, K-12 education is different; it is governed much differently, and it concerns parents and involves their children.

North American testing differs because North American education differs

The United States and Canada are large and diverse countries with federal systems of government comprising 50 states, the national capital District of Columbia, and associated territories in the former and 13 provinces and territories in the latter. Constitutionally, education is a state or provincial responsibility, although most states and the province of Ontario have delegated some authority to operate and finance elementary and secondary schools to over 12,000 local school districts.

The structure of higher education in North America is diverse as well, with nearly 1,600 public institutions and almost 2,000 private institutions offering a wide range of programs.

Across all the U.S. states, the proportion of public school funding at the primary and secondary level averages about an even split between state and local authorities, but the exact proportions vary

widely. One state, for example, provides less than ten percent of public school revenues, while another provides 90 percent. The federal government plays a very limited role in the governance of education, but provides some funding to states and school districts (about 7 percent of public school revenues), mostly to support programs for students with special educational needs. It also provides financial aid to postsecondary education students in the form of scholarships and loans.

The federal role in education in Canada is even smaller. Indeed, some would argue that, for most of Canada's history, there was no federal role in education outside of, say, the collection of education statistics. The Council of Ministers of Education of Canada (CMEC) was formed in 1967 to discuss matters of mutual interest, but it comprises the group of provincial and territorial education ministers, and is independent of the federal government. In its own words "CMEC provides leadership in education at the pan-Canadian and international levels and contributes to the fulfilment of the constitutional responsibility for education conferred on provinces and territories. CMEC is governed by an Agreed Memorandum approved by all members" (Retrieved June 23, 2007 from http://www.cmec.ca/abouteng.stm). It employs just 40 full-time staff.

Arguably, CMEC has become most active in developing statistical indicators and assessments. Most provinces have participated independently in the International Assessment of Educational Progress (IAEP) in 1991, in the Third International Mathematics and Science Study (TIMSS) in 1995, and in the Programme for International Student Assessment (PISA) in more recent years. Between 1993 and 2004, the CMEC sponsored the School Achievement Indicators Program (SAIP), a cyclical program of pan-Canadian assessments of student achievement in mathematics, reading and writing, and science. It has since been replaced by the Pan-Canadian Assessment Program (PCAP), which will continue to assess performance in the same three

core subjects as SAIP but will leave room for other subjects to be added as the need arises.

Like the U.S. NAEP, the PCAP is a system monitoring test. It draws a random sampling of schools in participating provinces and territories, within which only a random selection of 13- or 15-year-old students sit for the assessment.

Each state or province has its own standards for teacher education, which occurs, in most U.S. states at least, in a wide variety of higher education institutions. More than several U.S. states host over 100 separate higher education institutions accredited to train teachers. By comparison, some countries deliberately restrict the number of teacher-training institutions in order to more easily maintain quality control and curricular coherence.

Traditionally, U.S. public schools and most Canadian public schools, even at the upper secondary level, have generalized, not specialized. When each student attends school in his own town or neighborhood, the curricular offerings of each school appeals to as many student interests as possible within budget constraints. The result is often a watered-down or greatly abbreviated version of the less common arts and vocational-technical subjects, taught by generalist rather than specialist teachers. Articulation agreements between vocational-technical school programs and employers or crafts unions so common in Europe and East Asia have been uncommon in North America.

With the collapse in K-12 education standards in the 1960s and 1970s, many secondary schools attempted to model their curricular offerings along the lines of universities (where students chose their courses), offering a panoply of courses of widely varying rigor intended to please fickle students of any taste. Cynics would argue that the model followed was not the university, but the shopping mall. (Powell, Farrar & Cohen, 1985) Whatever the cause, the proliferation of *ad hoc* standards made testing a common curriculum impossible. Nationally norm-referenced tests are not good candidates for standards-based testing but, at the time, nothing better

(i.e., aligned to a prescribed curricula) was available in most of North America.

How North American students have it easy

A survey the Organisation for Economic Co-operation and Development (OECD) conducted of its member countries in 1990–1991 on the number and duration of their systemwide tests revealed that U.S. students faced fewer hours and fewer numbers of high-stakes standardized tests than their counterparts in every one of the 13 other countries and states and fewer hours of state-mandated tests than their counterparts in 12 of the 13 other countries and states (Phelps, 1996, 25).

In their classic eight-country set of case studies, Eckstein and Noah (1993, 149, 167) ranked the United States lowest both in "examination burden" and "examination difficulty."

In their seven-country survey of secondary school math and science examinations, Britton, Hawkins, and Gandal (1996, 202–203) asserted:

> While only 6.6 percent of US students take Advanced Placement (AP) examinations, roughly a quarter to a half of all students in other nations take and pass advanced subject-specific examinations.
>
> In each country except the United States, college-bound students seeking to study in a university must pass demanding, subject-specific examinations. In France, Germany, and Israel, even many students who do not go on to college take these examinations because they are a prestigious credential in their societies.

Finally, in a review of widely-available documentary source material, I found that, over the period 1974–1999, "In 31 countries and provinces, 59 large-scale, external testing programs were added, and only 5 were dropped." Other countries and provinces added 22 monitoring exams, 6 subject-area end-of-course testing programs, 2 primary-to-secondary-level achievement tests, and 2 diagnostic exams. Thirty tests with **medium-stakes** or high-stakes

Medium stakes test

partial or conditional consequences that are defined in law or regulations to result from exceeding, or not, one or more score thresholds.

were added, and only four dropped (Phelps 2000c, 17, 18).

Moreover, course requirements seem more difficult in other countries even in non-core subjects. It is not uncommon to hear of European students spending more years studying a fourth language than U.S. students spend studying a second. Given how much more time they have to learn them, one would assume that U.S. students would perform relatively better on international tests in the core subjects.

University admissions practices outside the United States

There are a number of ways students can enter higher education. Prospective students typically gain admission by accomplishing one or more of the following types of activities: completing secondary schooling or earning a degree or certificate from a secondary school; passing either an exit (from secondary school) or entrance (to a higher education institution) examination; taking additional class work; gaining experience in the desired area of study; or reaching other standards that are usually related to academics.

Because the systems of higher education vary both across and within countries, it is critical to recognize both variations in order to draw a more accurate picture of the process of admissions. The classification scheme in table 5 delineates countries where institutions have uniform national requirements; those where institution policies vary according to regional differences; those where individual institutions have their own requirements; and those that base acceptance on program-related standards.

Several patterns can be observed in table 5. Most of the selected countries include higher education institutions that uniformly require the completion of secondary school, a degree or a certificate, the maintenance of minimum academic standards, and the availability of alternative modes of university

TABLE 5: REQUIREMENTS FOR ADMISSION TO HIGHER EDUCATION, BY METHOD AND COUNTRY

	Completion of secondary/ degree or certificate	Upper secondary exit exam	Entrance exam	Commercial tests	Additional course work	Experience	Academic standards	Late or re-entry options for adults and dropouts
Australia	○	◆	●	●		●	◆	Yes
Canada	■	■	●	●	■			Yes
France	◆	◆	●		●		◆	Yes
Germany	○	◆	●			●		Yes
Italy	◆	◆					◆	Yes
Japan	◆	◆	◆,●					Yes
Russia	●		●				◆	Yes
Spain	◆		◆		◆		◆	
Sweden	◆	◆	●			●	◆	Yes
Switzerland	◆	●	■			○		
United Kingdom	◆	◆	●				◆	Yes
United States	◆	■	●	●			●	Yes

◆ Uniform national standard
● Institution standards for entry into higher education
○ Standards for entry into specific higher education program
■ Standards vary regionally

SOURCE: Phelps, Dietrich, Phillips, & McCormack, Higher education: An international perspective, p.72 http://www.thirdeducationgroup.org/Review/Resources/IntlHigherEducation.htm

entry for older, working adults who might not have graduated from secondary school in their youth. In addition, while most secondary school exit examinations are determined by government authorities in charge of secondary schools, at either a federal or regional level, entrance examinations are administered by individual institutions of higher education, or are nationally standardized tests that produce results that individual institutions may use as they wish. Furthermore, Canada, France, and Spain all

require additional classes of some kind, depending upon their higher education systems.

Since there are a variety of different kinds of schools and programs within higher education in every country, not all qualifying factors apply to every student. Students wishing to enter a vocational program usually complete secondary level vocational schooling, earn a certificate of a particular trade, and acquire the necessary experience (e.g., from an apprenticeship or internship) to continue in the same field. In Germany, for example, post-secondary trade or technical schools are open to students who did not follow the academic track in secondary school and, instead, earned a certificate from a vocational secondary school. Germany's dual system, and several technical secondary programs normally leading to placement in an occupation, do not preclude non-academic track students the opportunity to continue into post-secondary schooling.

Academically oriented higher education institutions, including universities, professional schools, and some advanced technical schools, have somewhat similar, yet distinct, requirements leading to admission. First, students must complete their secondary schooling in an academic track, or earn a certificate or degree. Second, admission often depends upon an entrance or exit examination, with these exams varying in level of standardization. While most entrance examinations are produced by the institutions of higher education themselves, commercially mass-produced tests, for example, are used as standardized entrance examinations for Australia and the United States (e.g., SAT, ACT). Secondary exit examinations are standardized across countries such as France, Germany, Japan, and Italy, but are regionally based in Switzerland and Canada. Finally, particular institutions and programs may require academic records or experiences that are related to the field of desired study. Universities in some countries (Germany and Italy for instance) admit students who did not follow the academic track in secondary school, however the students'

scores on their entrance examinations still must meet the academic standards of the university.

While the majority of students enter post-secondary schools in their late teens or early 20s, there are options for adults who did not complete their secondary schooling, who did not take the necessary exams for admission, or who otherwise chose not to attend. Countries either give adults the privilege to enter higher education by valuing their work experience, or classes are made available to prepare them for the required exit or entrance exams. In Japan, for example, the University Entrance Test Scheme helps adults who did not complete their upper-secondary school courses. German adults can attend the *Abendgymnasium,* evening school, to prepare for the *Abitur.* Swedish adults can take the Swedish SAT (or, SweSAT). (See also "DAEU: le diplôme de la seconde chance.")

The North American commercial testing industry

In the United States today, there exist several industrial clusters of test development:

- New York City-Princeton-Philadelphia loop (College Board, ERB, Vantage, TASA, Promissor, Thompson, ETS and some of the more high profile occupational licensors [e.g., LSAT, NBME])
- Midwestern quadrilateral of Iowa City (ACT, Iowa Tests, and Pearson), Lincoln-Omaha, Nebraska (Buros Center and Gallup), the Twin Cities (DRC, ASC, NCS), and Chicago (Riverside, SSI, STS)
- Monterrey-Sacramento axis (home to the original California Test Bureau [now CTB/McGraw-Hill], Defense Department language testing, and firms working on California state testing contracts)
- San Antonio-Austin axis (Harcourt-Psych Corp, PRO-ED, and various firms working on Texas state testing contracts)
- Washington, D.C., with many testing programs sponsored by the federal government (e.g., var-

ious military selection tests, the foreign-service exam) or trade and professional associations (e.g., the GED, the MCAT)

Aside from other testing firms scattered elsewhere, most other test development activity occurs in state capitals or in the testing and measurement departments of universities.

Educational test development by private commercial firms is almost uniquely a North American phenomenon. Elsewhere in the world, tests are developed by government education ministries, teachers associations, or higher education institutions. Even Cito, which retains an independent status and sometimes fulfills contracts outside its home country of the Netherlands, is, in effect, a quasi-governmental organization given its permanent role in developing the Dutch national examinations. SMART in Belgium and the U.K. examinations syndicates are housed in universities. The International Baccalaureate test developers in Cardiff, Wales stick to their own knitting. Indeed, any sales-driven marketing of test development services outside of North America is most likely to be North American in origin.

There exist hundreds of commercial test development firms in the United States. Some sell a niche product, for example, a single test or single test type, or a single service in the value chain of test development (e.g., scoring, results reporting). Others offer a comprehensive array of test products, that includes both achievement and aptitude tests, and educational, psychological, and certification exams.

In a 1993 book, a few outspoken critics of testing coined the term "fractured market" to describe the structure of the North American commercial testing industry. Don't bother looking in an economics text for the term; you won't find it there. Here's the definition from the coiners themselves:

> Different firms are engaged in different segments of the testing marketplace. And even for a single test, different organizations may be responsible for sponsoring, building, administering, scoring

and reporting that test. Also, while there have been a significant number of mergers and acquisitions among firms active in the testing marketplace over the last twenty years, it is clear from the new prominence of firms such as Scantron and Pro-Ed that the testing industry remains fluid enough to allow the successful entry of new players. And the rapid rise to eminence of firms such as NCS and Scantron shows that computer technology is having an increasing influence on the testing marketplace and that test-related services, such as scoring and reporting of results, are an increasingly important segment of the market, as compared with sales of tests themselves. (Haney, Madaus, & Lyons 2003, 54)

In other words, a "fractured" market was an ordinary, healthy, competitive market, the kind that serves consumers best. Why, then, was the book's final chapter devoted to "Mending the Fractured Marketplace?" Turns out, the lead author considered a "fractured market" to be a bad thing, and proposed centralized control and direct regulation of the testing industry.

Fast forward fifteen years, and the same fellow can be heard bemoaning an alleged paucity of competition and a concentrated market. "[the testing industry] is not entirely a monopoly, but it is an oligopoly, with very little regulation." (as quoted in Reichgott 2007; see also Toch 2007) (Ironically, some educators want to regulate the industry that produces the chief means for regulating them.)

There are two problems with his industry analysis, however. First, he is wrong about the oligopoly structure. (He is also wrong about a lack of regulation.) Second, oligopolies are not necessarily bad, anyway. Countless industries are both oligopolies and intensely competitive (e.g., soft drinks, wet shavers, consumer electronics batteries, enterprise software, aircraft engines, commercial aircraft). (see Mund & Wolf, 1971; Needham, 1969)

An industry becomes uncompetitive when the cost for potential competitors to enter the market is too high—typically caused by steep scale economies or large sunk costs (i.e. fixed investments). Test item

banks and networks of computer testing centers are sometimes cited as large fixed investments and barriers to entry in the testing business. But, these barriers may not be very high.

One might reasonably assume that the companies that have gone to all the trouble to build up geographically widespread networks of computer testing centers must have raised a high sunk cost-fixed investment barrier to new entrants in the growing computer testing market. Alternatively, one might assume, the two largest network operators—Pearson Vue and Thomson Prometric—should be able to charge "duopoly" prices for other companies' use of their networks.

The alleged Pearson-Thompson duopoly, however, proved to be no barrier to ACT, Inc., the company best known for its namesake college entrance test that also administers a large number of occupational certification tests by computer. ACT built its own continent-wide network of hundreds of computer testing centers by piggybacking off of postsecondary institutions. Most U.S. colleges maintain and manage their own computer testing centers for their own testing needs. These already-existing centers are supervised by trained test administrators, are heavily used by the colleges themselves at predictable times of year and, at other times, hold slack capacity that they are eager to sell or lease to testing companies like ACT.

In 2002, ETS phased out computer-based testing at 84 of 195 international centers. The affected test centers had been processing low volumes of tests and accounted for only 15 percent of international test takers. ETS's international CBT centers were run by Thomson Prometric. (International Directory of Company Histories) This would have been an odd business decision if testing center networks were considered dear, and a barrier to market entry.

Still, if the development of geographically widespread networks of computer testing centers does not represent a barrier to market entry, one might reasonably surmise that the development of large, proprietary item banks would. In 2006, the Texas

Education Agency chose to part company with National Evaluation Systems (NES), the firm that had held the state teacher certification testing contract for a dozen years. (At about the same time in the fluidly competitive testing market, NES won the teacher certification testing contract in Georgia that had long been held by ETS.) The new contractor, ETS, was awarded its contract only a few months before they would be required to administer the full panoply of certification tests.

The outgoing contractor had written and validated tens of thousands of test items for over 50 separate administrator and teacher pedagogy and subject-area tests. Each test and each test item was custom-developed with the active participation of committees of Texas teachers and professors to meet Texas' unique teacher and administrator certification standards. How could a new test contractor build in a few months what the previous contractor had taken over a decade to build?

They couldn't. But they didn't need to; the state of Texas owned the items.

Twenty to forty years ago, school systems purchased tests intact "off the shelf." Testing companies owned the tests and all the items used to build the tests. But, times have changed, and with standards-based tests the balance of control has shifted from commercial test publishers to government agencies. Government agencies issue "requests for proposals," bids from testing firms flood in, and the agencies often have their pick of the litter. If, at the end of the contract period, an agency is not happy with an incumbent contractor, they can yank the contract.

Probably the single most important recent innovation in relation, educational testing quality, fairness, and control in the United States has been the addition of managerial and technical expertise in state education agencies. At that level, it is possible to retain an adequate group of technically proficient testing experts, adept at screening, evaluating, administering, and interpreting tests, who are not "controlled by commercial publishers" or naïve about test results. They, along with governors and

legislatures, are currently calling the shots in educational testing. Some of the most important decisions affecting the design and content of the tests, the character of the testing industry, and the nature of its work, are today being made by state testing directors.

According to the aforementioned critics, however, psychometricians eschew state service for higher salaries in the private sector. (Toch, 2007) Thus, "Many state agencies simply don't have the capacity to scrutinize the work of their testing contractors closely."

Then, where have those psychometricians gone, one wonders? Many of them now work as consultants or as professors and consultants, and one can find many of them working on state technical advisory committees, reviewing test contractors' work. Typically, these panels wield veto power over virtually all technical aspects of the tests.

The test development business is competitive, and there continue to be new entrants. The Associated Press article (Reichgott) cited above claimed "The NCLB testing industry is dominated by four companies" and identified Harcourt, CTB/McGraw-Hill, Pearson, and Riverside, neglecting to mention Data Recognition Corporation, ETS, and other firms that, collectively, have managed the NCLB-related test development in over a dozen states (including, as of summer 2007, Alabama, California, Hawaii, Louisiana, New Jersey, Ohio, Oklahoma, Pennsylvania, and Puerto Rico). These firms entered the K-12 large-scale educational assessment market for the first time during the NCLB years. The NCLB Act may well have increased the K-12 educational testing workload overall, but in so doing attracted new firms to the market.

Anyone inclined to believe the complaint that the testing industry is overly concentrated should glance down the list of "Nonprint Resources" in the appendix. Among the entities listed are over 50 that develop tests for a living. And those several dozen comprise only a small proportion of the total number.

Most of those listed focus on the educational testing market. But, there also exist hundreds of other firms that specialize in psychological diagnostic and employment testing. Most of them could enter some part of the education testing market if they chose to. The subject matter may be different; but the work and the test development skills required are essentially the same. Any testing firm's single most important asset represents no barrier to market entry: it is the knowledge and expertise of its people, and people are highly mobile.

Over thirty years ago, the Russell Sage Foundation sponsored a book-length study of the standardized testing industry. (Holmen & Docter, 1972) Comparing the names and players, and their ranks in sales, to today's illustrates the industry's fluidity. Of the top six firms in 1972, only one, ETS, has survived intact; three have since either disappeared or been gobbled up by then-unforeseen competitors; and two of them combined. Of the 22 organizations listed as "medium-size" in 1972, less than half still exist. Of the several dozen testing firms listed in this book's appendix, only one dozen can be found in the 1972 list. Any market-restricting oligopoly worth its salt would have the power to stop coming-and-going at such a rapid rate.

The critic who complained of a loosy-goosy "fractured marketplace" fifteen years ago and an overly concentrated "oligopoly" recently even got the trend wrong. Two–three decades ago, large, proprietary item banks were far more important than they are today. Two–three decades ago, most school systems purchased tests directly from less than a dozen sellers. Today, public agencies dictate their test specifications to test development firms, hired to short-term contracts.

And, the agencies have many firms to choose from. It is probably true that larger states limit themselves to a dozen or so possible bidders when they choose to bundle all of their testing work into a single contract. But, they do not have to assemble the work that way. More and more, states are split-

ting up their testing work among multiple contracts, and multiple contractors.

U.S. participation in international assessments

There are perhaps no singular events that elicit more public judgment of the quality of U.S. elementary and secondary education than the periodic release of results from international student assessments. The United States has participated in several international assessments of student achievement in mathematics, science, reading, civics, and other subjects since the 1960s. On most of these occasions, the comparison of U.S. student performance to their international counterparts' has provoked widespread interest from researchers, policy makers, and the public at large. The comparisons have prompted wholesale critiques and defenses of the U.S. education system in the popular press. The scholarly press, in the meantime, has filled with studies of U.S. relative achievement in the context of various background factors, such as the average **educational attainment** level or socioeconomic status of the test-takers' parents or the level of public education funding.

Educational attainment

the highest grade, year, or level of school attended and completed.

Some attention has focused on the validity of country-average test score comparisons in the light of differences in the mechanics of test administrations and sample selection across countries, with critics claiming that the differences nullify valid comparisons. Defenders of the country-average test score comparisons have argued that the differences in the test administration mechanics do not invalidate comparisons because they are not large enough or they should average out over time. They argue that comparative U.S. mathematics and science performance has been relatively consistent over multiple assessments and three decades.

The background analyses probing the deepest have se arched for explanations of relative achievement in the curriculum of each country. The Second International Mathematics and Science Study (SIMSS) in the early 1980s spawned *The Underachieving Curriculum,* a critique of the prevailing U.S. mathe-

matics curriculum written by some of the U.S. researchers directly involved in building and analyzing the SIMSS database (McKnight et al., 1987). Some of the same researchers were involved in building and analyzing the database for the Third International Mathematics and Science Study (TIMSS), administered in the 1994–1995 school year. Their curriculum analyses, *A Splintered Vision: An Investigation of U.S. Science and Mathematics Education, Many Visions, Many Aims: A Cross-National Investigation of Curricular Intentions in School Mathematics,* and *Characterizing Pedagogical Flow: An Investigation of Mathematics and Science Teaching,* echoed the critical refrain of *Underachieving Curriculum* (Schmidt et al. 1996a, 1996b, 1997). The U.S. mathematics curriculum, by comparison with its international counterparts, lacked focus and depth, they argued. One of the most widely quoted phrases characterized the U.S. math curriculum as "a mile wide and an inch deep."

Other studies have looked deeply at instructional practices across countries. Over two decades, Harold Stevenson and James Stigler (1992) observed and compared classroom culture and instructional practices in the United States and East Asian countries and have discovered some highly enlightening contrasts. Coincident with the TIMSS, George Stigler videotaped many hours of secondary-level mathematics classroom instruction in samples of German, Japanese, and U.S. schools. The contrasts in instructional style, demeanor, and content are striking (U.S. Department of Education, 1996).

Still other studies have looked more explicitly at the benefits, methods, and feasibility of benchmarking curricular and instructional practices across countries. To this effort, some researchers have focused on content standards (Resnick, Nolan, & Resnick, 1995; Nolan, 1997; Louis & Versloot, 1996) and others on performance standards (Britton & Raizen, 1996; Eckstein & Noah, 1993; Gandal, 1997; Stevenson & Lee, 1997). Still other researchers have argued for more comprehensive comparisons of education systems across countries and the impact of many systemic influences on curriculum and

instruction (Bishop, 1997; Mullis, 1997a), or they have advocated efforts toward benchmarking entire systems of curriculum and instruction (Cross & Stempel, 1995; Shanker, 1996; U.S. Department of Education, 1995).

The Third International Mathematics and Science Study (TIMSS)

The TIMSS, administered in 1994–1995, was the largest such assessment ever, with more than 40 countries participating at one or more of three grade levels—the rough equivalents of our 4th, 8th, and 12th grades. Results for the grade level at which the most countries participated—8th grade—were released first.

When the mathematics performance of U.S. 8th graders was compared to their international counterparts' in the summer of 1996, it seemed to reaffirm in the minds of many U.S. observers the legacy of pessimism from earlier international assessments. Among the 40 countries with student scores meeting minimal statistical requirements for comparison, U.S. 8th graders scored lower than 8th graders in 20 other countries and higher than those in only 7, when measured by a multiple comparison procedure involving all participating countries. U.S. students' scores were on a par with those of students in 13 remaining countries (Beaton, 1996, 23).

The performance of U.S. 4th graders, made public the following summer, seemed much better. A multiple comparison procedure showed U.S. 4th graders scoring below their counterparts in 7 countries, above those in 12, and on a par with those in 6 other countries (Mullis, 1997b, 25).

In between the relatively strong U.S. 4th-grade performance and the relatively weak U.S. 8th-grade performance were three grade levels and a steep decline in U.S. relative performance. Among all the 25 countries that participated at both the 4th- and 8th-grade levels and met minimal statistical requirements for comparison, the "synthetic gain" in mathematics achievement between the 4th and 8th

grades appeared to be the smallest in the United States (Mullis, 1997b, 43). One could speculate that the longer students stayed in U.S. schools, the less they learned, by comparison with average academic progress in other education systems.

The release of the 12th-grade results in 1998 only seemed to confirm the most pessimistic predictions. The unfortunate trend in relative U.S. student performance continued downward through the upper secondary years (Mullis et al., 1998).

Coincident with the student performance comparisons of the past decade, several groups studied the curricula of other countries and compared them with curricula typically found in the United States. Most commonly, these studies focused on the content of mandated, large-scale examinations as the most concise representations of a curriculum. Under Secretary Lynn Cheney in 1991, the National Endowment for the Humanities translated and published side-by-side comparisons of secondary-level history examinations from France, Germany, Japan, England and Wales, and Belgium (National Endowment for the Humanities, 1991). The National Center for Improving Science Education translated and compared several countries' science examinations (Britton & Raizen, 1996). The American Federation of Teachers did the same in several subject areas (e.g., American Federation of Teachers 1995a, 1995b). By most comparisons, the U.S. examinations looked easy.

Defenders of the *status quo* argued, validly, that the relative U.S. performance on international tests in subjects other than mathematics or science (e.g., in reading, civics) tends to be better. Other defenses were not as convincing. For example, some argued that the U.S. was disadvantaged by its ethnic heterogeneity, not noticing that most nations scoring higher were just as or more diverse (e.g., Australia, Canada, France, Hong Kong, the Netherlands, Singapore), or that if one compared the performance of our top kids to other countries' average kids, the U.S. performance did not look so bad, neglecting to mention that the U.S. looked bad in any apples-to-

apples comparison (e.g., our best to their best, our average to their average, our poorest to their poorest).

As if to ram home the point about the perennially poor U.S. performance in mathematics and science, however, the U.S. Department of Education officials announced in 2007 that the United States would not participate in the first TIMSS for physics and calculus since 1995, citing both a shortage of funds and students; there were not enough U.S. high school physics and calculus classes to form a statistically valid sample.

Lessons for the United States

Ina Mullis, of the U.S. International TIMSS Center, observed that the top-performing countries at the 8th-grade level were more likely to have high-stakes examination systems (Mullis 1997a).

The top-performing countries in the TIMSS made more use of other quality control measures as well, such as selection for curricular tracks, ability grouping, and other devices considered anathema by many U.S. education professors. All other factors being equal, quality control must be more difficult in the absence of common standards. One study of top-performing countries suggests that the most successful quality control efforts manage rather thoroughly the entire chain of elements that make up the curriculum and instruction system. (Phelps, 2001)

David F. Labaree (1999, 19) offered several compelling reasons for "the chronic failure of curriculum reform" in the U. S. schools:

> Loose coupling of school systems: . . . Administrators have little power to make teachers toe the line instructionally [because they] can fire teachers only with the greatest difficulty, and pay levels are based on years of service and graduate credits, not job performance.
>
> Adaptability of the school system: . . . Teachers adopt the language and the feel of a reform effort without altering the basic way they do things [and] the differentiation of subjects frees schools

to adopt new programs and courses by the simple process of addition. . . . They can always tack on another segment in the already fragmented curriculum [without changing any of the rest].

Weak links between teaching and learning: . . . Students, after all, are willful actors who learn only what they choose to learn. . . . The law says they have to attend school until they are 16 years old; the job market pressures them to stay in school even longer than that. . . . But these forces guarantee only attendance, not engagement in the learning process.

Note that these problems either do not exist or are less critical in highly integrated systems with many enforced quality controls, where reforms to a required, core curriculum cannot just be tacked on as an elective and students must listen and study if they wish to graduate. It could be that U.S. reforms in the past have faded before they reached the student due to poor quality control in curriculum and instruction systems that were not fully integrated.

Trends and convergence

Twelve countries participated in the First International Mathematics Study (FIMS) in 1964 and nineteen in the First International Science Study (FISS) in 1970. By contrast, over sixty jurisdictions were expected to participate in the International Association for the Evaluation of Educational Achievement's (IEA's) Trends in International Mathematics and Science Study (TIMSS) in 2007. As many or more are expected to join the Organisation for Economic Co-operation and Development's (OECD's) Programme for International Student Assessment (PISA) in 2009. International assessments are operationally and technically challenging (e.g., requiring **back translation**), and very expensive. Nonetheless, their popularity keeps growing.

As nations learn more about each others' education and assessment systems, they are more inclined to adopt their better features, and systems become more alike. For example, other countries have adopted some North American innovations, such as the multiple-choice item format, machine-scoring,

Back translation

a second and independent translation of a test from a second language to a first language that follows an earlier translation from the first, original language of the test to the second language; the degree to which a back translation matches the original test provides a measure of the accuracy of the original translation.

and large-scale diagnostic aptitude testing. North America has increased its use of more expository formats, standards-based content, and teacher involvement in developing and scoring tests. Moreover, while other countries now complement their high-stakes testing programs with low-stakes diagnostic assessments, North Americans now complement their low-stakes diagnostic assessments with high-stakes, standards-based testing.

GLOSSARY

Achievement (or, educational achievement)—the accumulated knowledge and skills acquired from previous learning.

Achievement test—designed to measure what has been learned, rather than to predict future performance.

Age-equivalent score—the chronological age in a defined population for which a given score is the median (middle) score.

Aptitude test—designed to predict how much you might learn in the future.

Aptitude—potential for future learning.

Assessment—generally refers to large-scale, systemwide measurement programs for pupil diagnosis, program evaluation, accountability, resource allocation, or teacher evaluation.

Back translation—a second and independent translation of a test from a second language to a first language that follows an earlier translation from the first, original language of the test to the second language; the degree to which a back translation matches the original test provides a measure of the accuracy of the original translation.

Criterion-referenced test (CRT)—a test that allows its users to interpret scores in relationship to a functional performance level, for example, the degree of competence attained by a particular student, without reference to the performance of others.

Diagnostic test—its purpose is to ascertain, prior to instruction, a student's abilities and level of achievement so that instruction might be adjusted appropriately.

Educational attainment—the highest grade, year, or level of school attended and completed.

Enacted curriculum—the subject matter content that actually is taught in the schools regardless of original intentions.

End-of-level test—test administered at the end of an educational level, such as primary or secondary.

Intelligence Quotient (IQ)—a unit for expressing the results of an intelligence test, based on the ratio of an individual's mental age (MA), as determined by the test, to their chronological age (CA): IQ = MA/CA x 100.

Intelligence test—test designed to measure an individual's level of cognitive functioning not related to any particular subject matter.

Intended curriculum—the subject matter content that is planned for school instruction, according to legislated and/or published standards.

Mean—the arithmetic average of a set of scores (i.e. the sum of a set of scores divided by their number).

Medium stakes test—partial or conditional consequences that are defined in law or regulations to result from exceeding, or not, one or more score thresholds.

Mental age—a unit for expressing the results of intelligence tests based on comparing the individual's performance on the test with the average performance of individuals in a specific chronological age group.

Minimum competency test—a high-stakes test that requires performance at or above a single threshold test score before certain educational attainment will be recognized.

Norms—the results of a test administered to a "norm group"—a representative sample of a larger population of interest.

Performance standards—specify the level or levels of achievement expected.

Power test—test administered with no effective time limit.

Raw score—the unadjusted score on a test, perhaps the simple number of correct responses, with no accounting for variations in item difficulty or weighting.

Scale score—the result of the mapping of a raw test score onto a more meaningful, interpretable, or comparable scale.

Selection—choosing individuals based, in whole or in part, on their test score (e.g., for university admission, a scholarship, employment).

Speeded test—test administered within a time limit such that some test takers may not finish.

Standard deviation—the square root of the average squared deviation around the mean (i.e., the variance). It is used as a measure of variability in a distribution of scores.

Summative assessment—when achievement tests are used to summarize the accumulation of knowledge up to that point.

Systemwide test—any test that is administered to all students or to a representative sample of all students within a jurisdiction for at least one grade level.

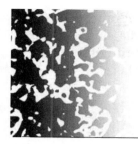

The Effects of Testing

From the 1950s through the 1970s, most U. S. states and Canadian provinces maintained rather innocuous testing programs if, indeed, they maintained any testing program at all. The Provinces of Québec and Newfoundland and New York State were notable exceptions, with well-developed programs that spanned the levels of education from the primary through the end of the secondary grades. All three jurisdictions administered elementary level monitoring tests and secondary-level **end-of-course exams**. Their secondary-level examinations counted for something—half of course grades in Québec and Newfoundland and a more prestigious diploma in New York State tied to test performance. (Tinkelman, 1965; U.S. GAO, 1993a)

At the same time, few other states or provinces administered high-stakes examinations, and most states and provinces administered no tests system-wide. Most of the states with testing programs simply purchased commercial norm-referenced tests "off the shelf" or required or suggested that school

End-of-course test

test administered at the end of a course of study, such as that for algebra I or chemistry.

districts do so. These tests were administered ostensibly for system monitoring or diagnostic purposes. Aggregate results from these test administrations may or may not have been publicized.

John Jacob Cannell
and the Lake Wobegon reports

In the 1980s, a West Virginia physician, John Jacob Cannell, was surprised that his state's students kept scoring "above the national average" on a national norm-referenced standardized test (NRT), given the state's low relative standing on other measures of academic performance. He surveyed the situation in other states and with other NRTs and discovered that the students in every state were "above the national average," on achievement tests, according to their norm-referenced test scores.

In 1987, Cannell published the results of his study, *Nationally Normed Elementary Achievement Testing in America's Public Schools.* The phenomenon was dubbed the **Lake Wobegon Effect**, in tribute to the mythical radio comedy community of Lake Wobegon, where "all the children are above average." The Cannell report implied that half the school superintendents in the country were lying about their schools' academic achievement. It further implied that, with poorer results, the other half might lie, too.

Lake Wobegon effect

score inflation or artificial test score gains.

School districts could purchase NRTs intact from commercial test publishers and administer them on their own. With no "external" test administrators watching, school and district administrators were free to manipulate any and all aspects of the tests. They could look at the test items beforehand, and let their teachers look at them, too. They could give students as much time to finish as they felt like giving them. They could use the same test form year after year. They could even score the tests themselves. The results from these internally-administered standardized tests primed many a press release.

Cannell followed up with a second report (1989), *How Public Educators Cheat on Standardized Achievement Tests,* in which he added similar state-by-state information for the secondary grades. He also summarized the results of a survey of test security practices in the 50 states, and printed some of the feedback he received from teachers in response to an advertisement his organization had placed in the newspaper *Education Week* in the spring of 1989 (see chapter 3).

The natural response to widespread cheating in most non-education fields would be to tighten security and to transfer the evaluative function to an external agency or agencies—agencies with no, or at least fewer, conflicts of interest. That is how testing with stakes has been organized in hundreds of other countries for decades.

Steps in this direction have been taken in the United States, too, since publication of Cannell's Reports. For example, it is now more common for state agencies, and less common for school districts, to administer tests with stakes. In most cases, this trend has paralleled both a tightening of test security and greater transparency in test development and administration.

Long ago, education officials could administer a test statewide and then keep virtually all the results to themselves. In those days, those education officials with their fingers on the score reports could look at the summary results first, before deciding whether or not to make them public. Few reporters then even covered systemwide, and mostly diagnostic, testing much less knew when the results arrived at the state education department offices. But, again, this was long ago.

Legislative responses

Between then and now, both California (in 1978) and New York State (in 1979) passed "truth in testing" laws that give individual students, or their parents, access to the corrected answers from standardized tests, not just their scores. The laws also

require test developers to submit technical reports, specifying how they determined their test's reliability and validity, and they require schools to explain the meaning of the test scores to individual students and their parents, while maintaining the privacy of all individual student test results.

Between then and now, the U.S. Congress passed the Family Education Rights and Privacy Act (FERPA), also called the Buckley Amendment (after the sponsor, Congressman James Buckley [NY]), which gives individual students and their parents nationwide similar rights of access to test information and assurances of privacy. Some federal legislation concerning those with disabilities has also enhanced individual students' and parents' rights to test information (e.g., the Rehabilitation Act of 1973).

Judicial responses

Moreover, the courts, both state and federal, have rendered verdicts that further regulate the development and use of standardized tests. *Debra P. v. Turlington* (1981) is a case in point (Debra P. being a Florida student and Mr. Turlington being Florida's education superintendent at the time). A high school student who failed a nationally-norm-referenced high school graduation examination sued, employing the argument that it was not constitutional for the state to deny her a diploma based on her performance on a test that was not aligned to her school's curriculum. In fairness, she argued, students should have an opportunity to learn in school what they must show they have learned on a graduation test. In one of the most influential legal cases in U.S. education history, the court sided with Debra P. against the Florida Education Department.

The court declared it unfair to impose negative consequences, such as retention in grade or diploma denial, on students who fail tests based on pseudo-curricula, rather than the curriculum to which they actually were exposed. This principle has since been written into the *Standards for educational and psy-*

chological testing and now virtually all grade-promotion and graduation examinations are standards-based, not nationally norm-referenced, and achievement, not aptitude, tests.

A more recent and even higher profile case (*GI Forum v. Texas Education Agency,* (2000)), however, reaffirmed that students still must pass a state-mandated test to graduate, if state law stipulates that they must (Phillips, 1996, 2000).

U.S. state and federal judges in the past few decades have rendered many verdicts affecting standardized tests' content, administration, and use. Moreover, their decisions cover the full range of test types, with important cases concerning intelligence testing (e.g., *Larry P. v. Riles*), educational and psychological diagnosis (e.g., *Pennsylvania Assn. for Retarded Children v. Commonwealth of Pennsylvania*), university admissions (e.g., *Regents of the State of California v. Bakke*), employment (e.g., *Detroit Edison Co. v. National Labor Relations Board*), and occupational licensing (e.g., *Bartlett v. New York State Board of Law Examiners*) (Buckendahl & Hunt, 2005).

Response of the professions

Cannell's public-spirited work, and the shock and embarrassment resulting from his findings within the psychometric world, likely gave a big push to reform as well. The industry bible, the **Standards for Educational and Psychological Testing**, mushroomed in size between its 1985 and 1999 editions, and now consists of 264 individual standards (i.e., rules, guidelines, or instructions) (American Educational Research Association, American Psychological Association, & National Council on Measurement in Education, 1999, 4, 5):

Standards for Educational and Psychological Testing

produced by the APA, NCME, and AERA; have become the de facto regulations governing legal uses and administration of most standardized tests in the United States.

> The number of standards has increased from the 1985 Standards for a variety of reasons. . . . Standards dealing with important nontechnical issues, such as avoiding conflicts of interest and equitable treatment of all test takers, have been added . . . such topics have not been addressed in prior versions of the Standards.

The *Standards* now comprise 123 individual standards related to test construction, evaluation, and documentation, 48 individual standards on fairness issues, and 93 individual standards on the various kinds of testing applications (e.g., credentialing, diagnosis, and educational assessment). Close to a hundred member and research organizations, government agencies, and test development firms sponsor the development of the *Standards* and pledge to honor them.

Any more, to be legally defensible, the development, administration, and reporting of a high-stakes test must adhere to the *Standards* which, technically, are neither laws nor government regulations but are, nonetheless, regarded in law and practice as if they were. (Buckendahl & Hunt, 2005).

Moreover, technical standards for test development and administration have been composed or endorsed by dozens of other professional organizations, including the International Test Commission, the American Counseling Association, the Association of Test Publishers, the International Personnel Management Association, the National Association of College Admission Counselors, and the Society of Industrial and Organizational Psychology. (Buckendahl & Hunt, 2005; Geisinger, 2005; O'Boyle & McDaniel, 2007; Phelps 2007b; Plake, 2005). Standards documents are revised and updated as needed. Piling all the standards documents on one spot would build a tower thousands of pages tall.

Some critics of standardized testing seem to be unaware of both the extent of the technical safeguards and the imperative that test developers follow them. Indeed, some persistent criticisms were answered by psychometricians long ago, and written into one or more set of technical standards which have, in turn, been followed scrupulously by test developers for years.

This is not to say that test developers do not sometimes make mistakes—we all do—or sometimes try to cut corners too sharply under budget pressure. But, some of the accusations proffered by critics become, over time, more outdated and far-

fetched. (See, for example, Camara, 2007; Carlson & Geisinger, 2007; Goodman & Hambleton, 2005; Gottfredson, 2007; Leighton, 2007; Lohman, 2006; McRae, 2006; O'Boyle & McDaniel, 2007; Phelps 2007c; and Sireci & Hambleton, 2007)

Education researchers' response

The Cannell Reports attracted a flurry of research papers, too, mostly from critics of testing. Most researchers concurred that the Lake Wobegon Effect was real—across most states, many districts, and most grade levels, more aggregate average test scores were above average than would have been expected by chance—many more. Cannell had found evidence of **test-score pollution** on a massive scale.

But, what caused the Lake Wobegon Effect? In his first (1987) report, Cannell named most of the prime suspects—educator dishonesty (i.e., cheating) and conflict of interest, lax test security, inadequate or outdated norms, inappropriate populations tested (e.g., low-achieving students used as the norm group, or excluded from the operational test administration), and teaching the test.

In a table that "summarizes the explanations given for spuriously high scores," one prominent testing opponent provided a cross-tabulation of alleged causes with the names of researchers who had cited them (Shepard, 1990, 16). Conspicuous in their absence from the table, however, were Cannell's two primary suspects—educator dishonesty and lax test security. This research framework presaged what was to come. The Lake Wobegon Effect continued to receive considerable attention and study from mainstream education researchers, but Cannell's main points—that educator cheating was rampant and test security inadequate—were dismissed out of hand, and persistently ignored thereafter (See, for example, Baker, 2000; Greene, Winters, & Forster, 2003, 2004; Koretz, 1996; Koretz, 1991; Linn, 2000; Linn, Graue, & Sanders, 1990; Shepard, 2000). In statistical jargon, this is called "left-out variable bias" (LOVB).

Test score pollution

term coined by Haladyna, Nolen, and Haas (1991), derived from earlier work by Messick (1984), that "refers to factors affecting the truthfulness of a test score interpretation. Specifically, pollution increases or decreases test performance without connection to the construct represented by the test, producing construct-irrelevant test score variance."

For two decades now, testing critics have insisted that high-stakes, and not educator cheating or lax security, were responsible for Cannell's artificial test score gains, despite the fact that only one of the dozens of Cannell's score-inflated tests had any stakes attached (Phelps, 2005e). They identify "teaching to the test" (i.e., test preparation or test coaching) as the direct mechanism that produces this test **score inflation** (Crocker, 2005).

The reasoning goes like this: under pressure to raise test scores, teachers "narrow the curriculum" to comprise only subject matter that will be covered on the test and teach to the test. Moreover, teachers reduce the amount of time devoted to regular instruction and, instead, focus on test preparation that can be subject-matter free. This behavior, they argue, leads to **unintended consequences**: test scores rise, but students learn less.

Unfortunately for their claims, research conducted on this hypothesis shows that the strategy doesn't work. Apparently, teachers who spend more than a brief amount of time focused on test preparation do their students more harm than good. Their students score lower on the tests than do other students whose teachers eschew any test preparation beyond simple format familiarization (and, instead, use the time for regular subject-matter instruction) (see, for example, Palmer, 2002; Crocker, 2005; Camara, 2007). Moreover, students who know the specific content of prep tests beforehand tend to study less, learn less, and score lower on final exams than those who do not (see, for example, Tuckman, 1994; Tuckman & Trimble, 1997).

Score inflation

a rise in test scores over time that is not caused by a genuine increase in the quality being measured, such as academic achievement.

Unintended consequences

another way of saying that standardized testing may portend adverse effects (e.g., students who score poorly might get hurt feelings, or be held back a grade).

The "high stakes cause test-score inflation" myth

In fact, a deliberate reading of Cannell's reports reveals that low, not high, stakes were most often associated with test-score inflation. Granted, students and educators would probably be found more likely to cut corners or cheat on a test if the stakes of a test could be isolated from all other characteristics of a test administration. In reality, however,

the stakes can never be isolated from all other factors, such as test security. Other factors are always present; ergo, the only meaningful effects-of-testing studies consider the *multi-variate* context.

Low-stakes tests make cheating possible because they are often administered with lax (or no) security. Conversely, high-stakes tests are more likely to produce reliable test results because those tests are typically administered with tighter security. Given current law and practice, the typical high-stakes test is virtually certain to be accompanied by **item rotation**, sealed packets, monitoring by external proctors, and the other test-security measures itemized as necessary by Cannell in his late-1980s appeal to clean up the rampant corruption in educational testing and reporting.

Other test-security enhancements common to high-stakes tests include a high public profile, media attention, and voluntary insider (be it student, parent, or educator) surveillance and reporting of cheating. Do a Web search of stories about test cheating, and one finds that, in many cases, cheating educators were turned in by colleagues, students, or parents. Public attention does not induce otherwise honest educators to cheat, as testing critics have claimed. The public attention enables otherwise successful cheaters to be caught. Under current law and practice, it is typically high-stakes tests that are public, transparent, and explicit in their test attributes and public objectives, and it is typically low-stakes tests that are not.

As it happens, the states that inflated their norm-referenced test scores in the 1980s were mostly Southern and suffered low academic reputations. (By contrast, administrators in Northern and Western states may have been less inclined to cheat as they were already, and genuinely, above the national average in state-by-state comparisons.) Some of these states also administered high-stakes standards-based tests. Administrators may well have wanted to manipulate the scores on their standards-based tests, too. But, due to tighter security, they could not. Moreover, scores on the high-stakes standards-based

Item rotation

for tests that are administered periodically, the process of replacing some number of already-used test items with others that have similar content and statistical characteristics.

tests were generally not equated to any national academic achievement scales, so inflating their scores would have had little effect on boosting their states' (or their own) reputations.

Moreover, the Lake Wobegon states inflated their low-stakes norm-referenced test (NRT) scores whether or not they also maintained a separate high-stakes testing program. By any measure, Cannell's own state of West Virginia had terribly inflated NRT scores, but it had no high-stakes testing program. The same was true at the time for the neighboring state of Kentucky. Meanwhile, the states of Mississippi, North Carolina, and Arkansas also exhibited strong score inflation with their low-stakes NRTs, but all three states ran separate high-stakes standards-based testing programs, with which they enforced tight test security protocols.

Cannell's data do not show that accountability tests cause, or are even associated with, test score inflation. Testimony that Cannell solicited from hundreds of educators across the country reinforced his wealth of empirical evidence in support of the notion that educator dishonesty and lax test security were constant companions of test score inflation, and that lax test security was more common with low-stakes tests (Cannell, 1989, chapter 3).

The Cannell reports remain our country's most compelling and enduring indictment of education system self-evaluation (For other interesting examples, see Blum, 2002; Durham, 2000, Hills, 1991; Newbart, 2007; O'Donoghue, 2006; Phelps, 1994, 2000b, 2005b, 2007a, 2007c; Stiggins & Conklin, 1992; Stone, 1995; Stricherz, 2001; USA Today, 2001; Wyatt, 2001; Woodruff & Ziomek, 2004b).

But, most education researchers are education system insiders, reticent to suggest that any educators could be capable of ill motive.

The most certain cure for test score inflation is tight test security and ample item rotation, which are common with externally-administered, high-stakes testing. An agency external to the local school district must be responsible for administering the tests under standardized, monitored, secure conditions, just the way it is done in hundreds of other countries (See, for example, American Federation of Teachers, 1995a; Britton, Hawkins, & Gandal, 1996; Eckstein & Noah, 1993; Phelps, 1996, 2000c, and 2001; Zeng, 1999). If the tests have stakes, students, parents, teachers, and policy makers are more likely to take them seriously, and adequate resources are more likely to be invested toward ensuring test quality and security.

Any test can be made a Lake Wobegon test. All that is needed is an absence of test security and item rotation and the slightest of temptations for (some) educators to cheat. How a test is administered determines whether it becomes a Lake Wobegon test (i.e., one with artificial score gains over time). Ultimately, the other characteristics of the test, such as its name, purpose, content, or format, are irrelevant.

Two quite different types of test administration prevent artificial test score gains (i.e., score inflation). One type has good security and ample item rotation, both of which are more common with high- than with low-stakes tests. The second type produces scores that are untraceable to schools or districts. Some system-monitoring and diagnostic tests administered to samples of students or classrooms bear this characteristic. Any test producing scores that *are* traceable to particular schools, districts, or states might be used to make their administrators look good, if security is lax.

Experience shows that it does not take much incentive to induce at least some education administrators to cheat on standardized tests. But, cheating requires means, motive, and opportunity. When external agencies administer a test under tight security (and with ample item rotation), local school administrators are denied both means and opportunity to cheat. With tight security and ample item rotation, there can be no test score inflation.

There were no stakes for anyone, including teachers, with (all but one of) Cannell's Lake Wobegon tests—and no external evaluation or oversight. The researchers who have insisted after the fact that stakes were involved have just made it up.

Education administrators cheated, or set things up so that teachers couldn't help but passively cheat (e.g., by giving them the same test form to use year after year), then reported the fake results, and then boasted. They did it because they wanted to and, more importantly, because they could. The motivation was not pressure, but greed. The cheating was made possible, indeed, by an absence of pressure.

The list that Cannell included in his 50-state survey of test security practices (1989, Appendix I) remains a useful reference. Jurisdictions wishing to avoid test score inflation should consider:

- enacting and enforcing formal, written, and detailed test security and test procedures policies.
- formally investigating all allegations of cheating.
- ensuring that educators cannot see test questions either before or after the actual test administration and enforcing consequences for those who try.
- reducing as much as practicable the exclusion of students from test administrations (e.g., special education students).
- employing technologies that reduce cheating (e.g., optical scanning, computerized variance analysis).
- holding and sealing test booklets in a secure environment until test time.
- keeping test booklets away from schools until test day.
- rotating items frequently.
- prohibiting teachers from looking at the tests, even during test administration.
- using outside test proctors.
- spiraling different forms of the same test (i.e., having different students in the same room getting tests with different question ordering) to discourage student answer copying.

To Cannell's list from twenty years ago, one might add practices that consider the added advan-

tages the Internet provides to those who cheat. Item rotation, for example, is essential to preserve the integrity of any test that is periodically administered, by reducing item exposure. It has become even more important given that any student can post (their recollection of) a test question on the Internet immediately after the conclusion of a test, thus aiding students taking the same test at a later date or in a more westerly time zone the same day. In test security jargon, this practice is called "braindumping."

Test coaching and teaching to the test

Testing opponents identify "teaching to the test" (i.e., test prep or test coaching) as the direct mechanism that produces test score inflation (and also "narrows the curriculum"), though they conducted no direct test of the hypothesis. They assumed it to be the direct cause, by default, just as they assumed high-stakes to be the indirect cause by default, after dismissing other possible causes out of hand.

If it were true that externally-administered, highly-secure, high-stakes tests could be "taught to," we should be able to find evidence of it in the experimental literature—in studies that test the coaching hypothesis directly. Such studies have most commonly focused on college admissions testing, where test preparation services comprise a large industry. The research literature (discussed below) reveals a consistent result: test coaching does have a positive, but extremely small, effect.

Two aspects of test preparation

Essentially, there are two separate aspects to test preparation—(1) format familiarity and (2) remedial instruction or review in subject matter mastery. Since commercial test prep courses (like those of Stanley Kaplan and the Princeton Review) are too short to make up for years of academic neglect and, thus, provide inadequate remedial help with subject matter mastery, what should one think of their ability to help students with format familiarity?

The most rigorous of the test coaching experiments in the research literature controlled the maximum number of other possible influential factors. Judging from their results, the only positive effect left from test prep courses seemed to be a familiarity with test item formats, such that coached examinees can process items on the operational test form more quickly and, thus, reach more test items. In other words, those who are already familiar with the test item structure and the wording of the test questions can move through a test more quickly than can those for whom all the material is fresh. This information, however, is available to anyone for free; one need not pay for a test prep course to gain this advantage (Powers, 1993, 30).

Test preparation company claims

The Princeton Review's advertising claims, in particular, go far beyond familiarizing students with test format of the ACT or SAT, however. The Princeton Review argues that one can do well on multiple-choice standardized tests without even understanding the subject matter being tested. They claim that they can increase students' test scores merely by helping them to understand how multiple-choice items are constructed. Are they correct?

The evidence they use to "prove" their case is in data of their own making (See, for example, Smyth, 1990). The Princeton Review, for example, gives some students practice SATs, scores them, then puts them through a course, after which they take a real SAT. They argue that the second SAT scores are hugely better. Even if one trusts that their data are accurate, however, it does not subtract out the effect of test familiarity. On average, students do better on the SAT just by taking it again. Indeed, simply retaking the SAT is a far less expensive way to familiarize oneself with the test.

According to Powers (1993, 29):

> When they have been asked to give their opinions, less than a majority of coached students have said they were satisfied with their score changes—for

example, 24% of those polled by Snedecor (1989) and 43% of those surveyed by Whitla (1988).

Moreover, the test preparation companies do not provide benefit-cost calculations in their claims. Any test preparation course costs money, and takes time. That time spent in a test preparation course represents an opportunity lost for studying on one's own in a manner that could be more focused, directed, and useful (Powers, 1993, 29).

Results of studies on test preparation

For decades, independent scholars have studied the effect of test preparation courses like those offered by Stanley Kaplan and the Princeton Review. Becker's (1990) meta-analysis of such studies, for example, found only marginal effects for test coaching for the SAT. Becker analyzed study outcomes in terms of some 20 study characteristics having to do with both study design and content of coaching studied. Like previous analysts, she found that coaching effects were larger for the mathematics section than for the verbal section. She did not find that duration of coaching was a strong predictor of the effects of coaching. Instead, she found that of all the coaching content variables she investigated, "item practice," (i.e., coaching in which participants were given practice on sample test items) had the strongest influence on coaching outcomes) (Becker, 1990).

Overall, Becker concluded that, among 21 published comparison studies, the effects of coaching were 0.09 standard deviations for the verbal section and 0.16 for the mathematics section. That is, just 9 points for the Verbal and 16 points for the Math on their 500 point scales. That's virtually nothing, and far, far less than Stanley Kaplan and the Princeton Review claim.

Research completed in November 1998 by Donald Powers and Donald Rock update the earlier studies of Becker and others with newer data about the minimal effects of coaching on the revised SAT, which was introduced in 1994 (See Camara, 1999, 2007).

The estimated effects of coaching reported in this study are remarkably consistent with previous research published in peer reviewed scientific journals, all of which are at odds with the very large claims by several commercial coaching firms. (see also Briggs, 2001; DerSimonian & Laird, 1983; Kulik, Bangert-Drowns, & Kulik, 1984; Messick and Jungeblut, 1981; Zehr, 2001)

In surveying the research literature on test coaching, Powers noticed two compelling trends: first, the more rigorous the study methodology, the smaller the effect found from commercial test preparation courses and, second (1993, 26):

> . . . simply doubling the effort . . . does not double the effect. Diminishing returns set in rather quickly, and the time needed to achieve average score increases that are much larger than the relatively small increases observed in typical programs rapidly approaches that of full-time schooling (Messick & Jungeblut, 1981). Becker (1991) also documented the relationship between duration of coaching and effects on SAT courses, noting a weaker association after controlling for differences in the kind of coaching and the study design.

Most test coaching studies find only small correlations with test score changes. Some testing opponents dismiss these studies without risking a debate by ignoring them or, if they cannot ignore them, by attributing the results to researchers' alleged self-interest. Most of the researchers involved, however, have had no ties to the testing organizations associated with the SAT or ACT tests.

Narrowing the curriculum

A corollary ill effect of high stakes, according to some, is curricular narrowing—valuable subjects that are not tested (e.g., art and music, maybe even social studies or science) will be ignored or slighted by test-obsessed teachers and school systems. A variation on this theme holds that, even within a subject that is taught, content coverage will be narrowed (or curricular depth made shallow) in order to conform to the content or style of the test.

It is a truism, however, that there is only so much instructional time available, and choices must be made as to how it is used (Unless, of course, extra hours are added, as sometimes occurs under accountability requirements). If important non-tested subjects are being dropped, either they, too, should be tested or, perhaps, educators and policymakers are signaling that, in a world of tough choices among competing priorities, some subjects must in fact take a backseat to others. A state or school system could add high-stakes tests in art, music, language, and civics, or any other subjects. Alternatively, they could genuinely enforce course distribution requirements.

Attaching high-stakes to tests in some subjects and not others would be interpreted by most as a signal that the former subjects are considered to be more important. Especially where students are sorely deficient in basic skills and need extra instruction in them, it is likely that few parents would object to such priorities. Survey results show clearly that the public wants students to master the basics skills first, before they go on to explore the rest of the possible curriculum (Farkus, Johnson, & Duffet, 1997; Johnson & Immerwahr, 1994). If that means spending more time on "the basics," so be it, the public seems to be saying.

The benefits of prediction

Arguably, the test attracting the most attention from critics over the years is the SAT, used, along with its counterpart, the ACT, by virtually all U.S. colleges in making admissions decisions. Some testing critics claim an ever-growing list of colleges dropping the admission test score requirement. They may neglect to mention, however, that few of them drop the requirement without attaching stringss (Milewski & Camara, 2002).

In most cases, students who choose to apply without submitting SAT or ACT scores must enclose additional proof of readiness, such as a graded writing sample, or submit to an on-campus interview. Even then, there is no guarantee that the absence of

a test score will not bias an application negatively. Besides, most of the colleges that waive the admissions test requirement do so only in extraordinary circumstances (e.g., disabilities, remote foreign residence) (telephone conversation with NACAC officials, August 14, 1998).

Still, the impact of the SAT and ACT is often overstated. The overwhelming majority of colleges are not selective, so a low admissions test score will rarely keep a student out of college. Even at the most selective colleges, test scores are seldom used alone by college admissions staff to make decisions. Typically, it is one of many factors that include a student's high school grade point average, extracurricular activities, recommendations, essays, and so on. When surveyed, however, admissions counselors rate the ACT or SAT score as a more reliable measure than these other indicators. The results of the National Association of College Admission Counselors' (NACAC) annual survey have been consistent for well over a decade.

> The top factors in the admission process continued to be (in order): grades in college preparatory courses, standardized admission tests, and overall high school grade point average. Class rank and the application essay placed fourth and fifth, while teacher/counselor recommendations were sixth. A student's demonstrated interest in attending an institution also constitutes a key "tip" factor in admission. (2006, 29)

By "grades in college preparatory courses" NACAC means grades in recognized standardized college prep courses or actual college courses:

> 'College prep courses' include Advanced Placement, International Baccalaureate, dual enrollment, and other advanced/college-level coursework. (NACAC, 37)

The measure of the benefit to the colleges of admission tests is their **predictive validity**. The statistical correlation between admission test scores and first-year college grades exceeds 40 percent. The correlation between admission test scores and other college outcomes, such as retention in grade, cumu-

Predictive validity

correlation between test scores and future performance.

lative grade-point average, and completion is also strong. (See, for example, Bridgeman, McCamley-Jenkins, & Ervin, 2000; Camara, 2007; Cole & Willingham, 1997; Hezlett, et al., 2001; Kobrin & Michel, 2006; Noble, 1991, 2004; Powers & Kaufman, 2002; Sawyer, 1985; Stricker, et al., 1994; Ziomek & Andrews, 1996)

The SAT or ACT predict between 5 and 10 percent of college academic performance, above and beyond what any and all other factors, such as high school grades, predict. A high school education costs society and a student's parents tens of thousands of dollars; ergo, it costs that much to accumulate a high school grade-point average. A college admission test costs about $40. Proportionally, an admission test's return on investment (i.e., its informational "bang for the buck") is enormous.

College admissions officers are not required to use the SAT or ACT. They use them because they believe, based on personal experience, that they provide valuable information.

The benefits of high stakes

Tests with consequences, or *stakes,* can induce beneficial **washback effects** (a.k.a. backwash effects) (See, for example, Cheng & Watanabe, 2004). A plethora of research studies demonstrates that students and candidates study more and take their studies more seriously (and, thus, learn more) when facing tests with stakes. Moreover, when test-takers wish to perform well, and their teachers wish to help them, they tend to focus their preparation on mastering that knowledge or those skills they judge will be covered by the test. This has the indirect, but usually beneficial, effect of increasing learning efficiency by aligning educational or training program curricula with known standards, benchmarks, and goals.

There exist dozens of studies providing experimental and other empirical support for the notion that tightening the standards-curriculum-test alignment is associated with genuine achievement test

Washback effect

when some aspect of a test given at one grade level has an effect on school, teacher, or student behavior in earlier grades (a.k.a. backwash effect).

score gains. Likewise, there exist hundreds of studies providing experimental and other empirical support for the notion that high-stakes-induced motivation is associated with genuine achievement test score gains (See Phelps 2005f).

For example, controlled experiments from the 1960s through the 1980s tested the effect of stakes on learning. Half of the students in a population were assigned to a course of study and told there would be a final exam with consequences (reward or punishment) riding on the results. The other half were assigned to the same course of study and told that their performance on the final exam would have no consequences. Generally, there were no incentives or consequences for the teachers. Guess which group of students studied harder and learned more?

From the 1960s to the 1990s, the field of personnel psychology (i.e., industrial- organizational psychology) produced an impressive body of technically advanced research on the costs and benefits of testing for personnel selection. Thousands of empirical studies were conducted in the United States alone demonstrating that a fairly general aptitude or achievement test is the best single predictor of performance for the overwhelming majority of jobs, better than any other factor that employers generally used in hiring. The estimated net benefits of using tests for personnel screening were huge (See, for example, Schmidt & Hunter, 1998).

The phrase "effective schools" pertains to schools with demonstrably superior academic success. An enormous literature has developed on the topic, continues to grow, and has reached a remarkable degree of consensus–effective schools focus strongly on academics, have strong principals who see themselves as academic leaders, maintain high academic standards, monitor academic progress closely and continuously, hold themselves accountable for academic achievement, and test frequently. The number of studies finding the same several traits making schools effective producers of high

achievement gains now number in the several hundreds.

Some reviews of the literature were assembled in the early 1980s, and include those by Purkey & Smith (1983); Murnane (1981); Averch et al., (1971); Edmonds (1979); McKenzie (1983); Clark, Lotto, & Astuto (1984); Northwest Regional Laboratory (1990); and Cotton (1995). Some recent studies have fractured among different sub-topics. One still frequently hears of program evaluations that reproduce the methods (and results) of the effective schools studies without their authors realizing it.

The research literature on the achievement benefits of testing

Despite some educators' lack of interest in, or outright suppression of, the evidence demonstrating high-stakes testing's beneficial achievement effects, over a thousand studies have managed to find their way into print. As one psychologist, writing in the 1980s, wrote:

> Research studies about the influences of tests began to appear in the literature in the early 1930s. (Milton, 1981)

I have found some older than that, including titles such as: "An examination of examinations," "Assessing students: How shall we know them?" "The effect on recall and recognition of the examination set in classroom situations," "How students study for three types of objective tests," and "An experimental study of the old and new types of examination: The effect of the examination set on memory."

Peruse the education research literature and one can find hundreds of articles with titles including phrases such as "the effects of testing on . . . ," "the impact of testing on . . . ," "the consequences of testing for. . . ."

Look a little deeper and one finds bibliographies, just from the 1970s, such as

- a review of research written in 1971 entitled "The effects of tests on students and schools" with 240 citations (Kirkland).
- a *Compendium of educational research, planning, evaluation and assessment activities* from 1977 with 60 citations that describes then-current research being conducted in state education departments (New Jersey Department of Education).
- *Minimal competency testing: Issues and procedures, an annotated bibliography,* with 28 entries from 1977 (Wildemuth).
- *Annotated bibliography on minimum competency testing,* from 1978 with 52 citations, apparently compiled by ERIC staffers.
- *Competency testing: An annotated bibliography* from 1978 with hundreds of citations to research just from the mid-1970s (Jackson & Battiste).
- *Competency testing: Bibliography,* from 1979, with 240 citations (Hawisher & Harper).
- an edited volume containing detailed descriptions of seven state evaluations of their minimum competency testing programs (Gorth & Perkins, 1979).

Those who have claimed a paucity of evidence for testing's achievement effects either have not looked very hard, or did not wish to find it. (See, for example, Barth, 2006; Cizek, 2001; Education Commission of the States, 2006; Figlio & Lucas, 2000; Hanushek & Raymond, 2002a, 2002b, 2003; Jacob, 2001, 2002, 2003; Koretz, 1996; Linn, 1993; Loveless, 2003; Mehrens, 1998; Nave, Miech, & Mosteller 2000; Olson, 2002; Roderick, Jacob, & Bryk 2002; Strauss, 2006)

Types of achievement benefit studies

The vast research literature on the effects of standardized testing comprises many examples of every possible type of study, including each of the following:

- **Controlled experiments** attempt to create two or more groups of people as similar as possible and treated the same except for the variation in a single treatment factor. Ideally, persons are assigned to their groups randomly. For example, one group, or "classroom," might be given graded tests throughout the period of a course while the other group is not. Then, the two groups' achievement gains at the end of the course would be compared. For another example, one group might be told that the final exam counts and the other group that it does not. In all but one of the controlled experiments that I have read about the introduction or suggestion of stakes apparently induced greater academic achievement.

- **Quasi-experimental designs** model experiments as closely as is practical. Perhaps the "control" and "treatment" groups already exist, rendering a true experimental design impractical. So, the researcher may gather information on the background characteristics of each group and try to statistically control them during the analysis of the data. Typically two or more groups are compared on some outcome measure, with only one of the groups having been exposed to high-stakes tests.

- **Multivariate analysis** typically employs data sets from large-scale national or international tests or from longitudinal studies. Researchers attempt to isolate the effect of a high stakes testing program on some outcome (e.g., academic achievement, wages or job security later in life), by statistically "controlling" other factors that could also influence the outcome. These analyses are cross-sectional (e.g., students from states or countries with high-stakes tests compared to their counterparts in the other states and countries) or longitudinal (e.g., change over time in achievement of each student or each student cohort).

- **Interrupted time series with shadow measure designs** are possible when a jurisdiction

has maintained, and continues to maintain, a measure of achievement different than a newly-introduced high-stakes measure. If the jurisdiction continues to administer a no-stakes test, for example, after the introduction of a separate high-stakes test, they then might observe an abrupt and sustained improvement in scores on the no-stakes test. The "interruption" in the time series is the moment when the high-stakes requirement was introduced.

- **Pre-Post studies** look at the change in a test's scores after stakes are attached to it. Say, a jurisdiction employed a measure without stakes and then, at some point, attached stakes to it. Other potentially influential factors must be statistically isolated.

- **Program evaluations** represent the most common type of study design, program evaluation being a catch-all term to describe holistic studies that incorporate a variety of methods. The techniques most commonly included in program evaluations are case studies, surveys (written or oral), structured interviews, reviews of administrative records, and site visits.

- **Benefit-cost studies** attempt to estimate the real-world (e.g., dollar) value of identified and measurable benefits and costs. The total amount of benefit minus the total amount of cost equals the net benefit.

Research summaries

Fortunately for those of us who lack the time to read a thousand scientific studies, some scholars have summarized groups of them, as literature reviews, research syntheses, and meta-analyses.

Meta-analysis is a type of research review that calculates a statistical summary measure of impact from a group of studies on the same topic. Meta-analyses of the experimental literature on the effects of testing include

- Locke and Latham's (2002) meta-analysis of three decades' experiments on motivation and

productivity (conclusion: clear performance targets and goal-setting to reach them substantially increase productivity).

- Bangert-Drowns, Kulik, and Kulik's (1991) meta analysis of 35 studies on the achievement effects of varying frequency of testing (conclusion: achievement gains are almost always higher with testing than without; the optimal amount is more than weekly).

- Kulik and Kulik's (1989) meta-analysis of 53 studies of the achievement effects of varying types and frequencies of feedback to students on their performance, tests being the most common form of feedback information (conclusion: the feedback from tests improves achievement substantially, not only by identifying and clarifying weaknesses but also in disabusing those students complacent due to overconfidence).

- Kulik and Kulik's (1987) meta-analysis of 49 studies of the achievement effects of **mastery testing** (i.e., testing as a part of mastery learning programs) (conclusion: mastery learning, and the testing that is an essential part of it, produces substantial achievement gains).

Research reviews of the experimental literature on the effects of testing include

- Guskey and Gates' (1986) research synthesis of 25 studies on mastery learning (conclusion: mastery learning produces substantial achievement gains).

- Natriello and Dornbusch's (1984) review of studies on the achievement effect of standards (conclusion: in general, higher standards lead to greater effort, in part because students tend to not take seriously work that adults do not seem to take seriously, but there are limits; set the standards too high and some students may not try).

- Staats' (1973) review of experiments on classroom reinforcement programs, some of which involved testing.

Mastery testing

when students are tested periodically for diagnosis as many times as necessary to prove mastery of the material. In mastery learning regimes, each student may progress at a different pace, but ends up in the same place, mastering the material.

- Carroll's (1955) review of experiments on language learning in the military, in government, and at universities (conclusion: the more intense the experience, the more rapid the learning, and testing helps to intensify the experience);
- Cameron and Pierce's (1994, 1996) and Tuckman's (1994) reviews of studies on the effects of a wide variety of "extrinsic motivators," usually revealing that extrinsic motivators tend to increase motivation.

Two literature reviews by Crooks (1988) and Kirkland (1971) survey some of the territory covered by the reviews above. Following is Crooks' (1998) summary (448–449) of the Bangert-Drowns, Kulik, and Kulik meta-analysis (1991) of the research literature on testing frequency (which incorporates the test/no test choice).

> The review by Bangert-Drowns et al. (1988) used data from 31 studies which: (a) were conducted in real classrooms, (b) had all groups receiving the same instruction except for varying frequencies of testing, (c) used conventional classroom tests, (d) did not have serious methodological flaws, and (e) used a summative end-of-course examination taken by all groups as a dependent variable. The course length ranged from 4 weeks to 18 weeks, but only 9 studies were of courses shorter than 10 weeks. Bangert-Drowns et al. reported their results in terms of effect size (difference in mean scores divided by standard deviation of the less frequently tested group).
>
> Overall, they found an effect size of 0.25 favoring the frequently tested group, representing a modest gain in examination performance associated with frequent testing.
>
> Overall, the evidence suggests that a moderate frequency of testing is desirable, and more frequent testing may produce further modest benefits. Groups that received no testing during the course were clearly disadvantaged, on average. Only four studies reported student attitudes towards instruction, but all favored more frequent testing, with a mean effect size of 0.59, a large effect.

Following is Crooks' summary (457–458) of the Kulik and Kulik meta-analysis of the research literature on mastery testing.

> Kulik and Kulik (1987) conducted a meta-analysis of studies of testing in mastery learning programs, analyzing data from 49 studies. Each study took place in real classrooms, provided results for both a class taught with a mastery testing requirement and a class taught without such a requirement, and was judged free of serious experimental bias. The studies varied in length from 1 to 32 weeks, with about half shorter than 10 weeks. . . .
>
> The mean effect size on summative, end-of-course examination performance was 0.54, a strong effect.
>
> Thus the results of research on mastery testing suggest that the sizeable benefits observed largely represent the combined effects of the benefits described in earlier sections from more frequent testing, from giving detailed feedback on their progress on a regular basis, and from setting high but attainable standards.

Following is Crooks' summary (Crooks, 1988, 448–450) of the Natriello and Dornbusch (1984) review of the research literature on the achievement effects of varying classroom evaluation techniques.

> . . . higher standards generally led to greater student effort and to students being more likely to attend class. . . . The weaker students, who are most at risk in high demand classrooms, may need considerable practical support and encouragement if they are to avoid disillusionment.
>
> Not surprisingly, . . . if students thought the evaluations of their work were not important or did not accurately reflect the level of their performance and effort, they were less likely to consider them worthy of effort.
>
> When student performance on achievement tests is the criterion, research has generally shown that higher standards lead to higher performance (e.g., Rosswork, 1977), although again a curvilinear relationship may be predicted.

In her 1971 research review, "The effects of tests on students and schools," Marjorie C. Kirkland, added the following:

Studies showed that systematic reporting of test results assisted students (ninth grade) in developing greater understanding of their interests, aptitudes, and achievements. This improvement in self-estimates of ability was greater for students who were characterized as having high self-regard than for those having low self-regard. (309–310)

In line with the above studies and others which he reviewed, Bloom (1968) concluded that learning must include both the student's subjective recognition of his competence and public recognition by the school or society.

Three studies (Keys, 1934; Kirkpatrick, 1934; Ross & Henry, 1939) indicated that the less able student profited more from frequent testing than the more able student. The less able student seemed to profit mainly from direction of his learning to specifics and from practice in selecting correct responses. . . . One finding would seem to encourage the continuance of periodic testing: at least 70% of the students in the Turney (1931), Keys (1934), and Ross and Henry (1939) studies favored frequent tests and felt the test helped them to learn more. (312)

. . . where standardized testing was suddenly introduced, as in the Navy (Cronbach, 1960; Stuit, 1947), an impact could be seen. The Navy program clearly demonstrated that tests are a powerful instrument for administrative control of a classroom. The tests showed which teachers were bringing their groups "up to the standard" so that administrators could take prompt remedial action. Such tests present a threat to the teacher. Even without the threat of discharge or reprimand, the desire to make a good impression would cause the teacher to make a greater effort to teach effectively and, in turn, result in the teacher putting pressure on students to work harder. (322)

In a 1997 summary of the cognitive psychology literature, Dempster (1997, 333) writes:

Research on the effects of testing on learning has made it abundantly clear that test, do more than simply test; they also promote learning, even when no corrective feedback is provided and when there are no further study opportunities. . . . This effect is also truly remarkable in the scope of its application. It has been found with all sorts of tests (e.g., multiple-choice, short-answer, essay) and with all sorts of learning material ranging from traditional

laboratory learning lists (e.g., unrelated word lists) to more ecologically valid material such as prose passages and arithmetic facts. In many cases, the effect has been strong.

Please note that virtually all of the many studies thus far mentioned under the heading "Research Summaries" are of but one type—controlled experiments. As many as they are, they represent only a small proportion of the research literature on the effects of standardized testing. There also exist other research summaries of many other research studies on the effects of standardized testing using other methods (Phelps, 2005d).

The vast research literature on the effects of standardized testing covers all of the essential characteristics of high-stakes standardized testing's relationship to achievement, for example:

- the effect of setting high standards on achievement.
- the effect of testing on achievement, rather than not testing.
- the relationship between the frequency of testing and achievement.
- the effect of detailed feedback on achievement.
- the effect of high-stakes testing on student, teacher, and administrator motivation.
- the effect of high-stakes on student, teacher, and administrator behavior, by contrast to low-stakes' effect.
- the effect of high-stakes testing on the alignment of curriculum and instruction.
- the effect of setting clear targets for performance on achievement.
- the learning effect of test-taking itself.
- the firm conviction of all concerned–students, parents, the public, teachers, administrators, employers–that high-stakes testing induces students to study and learn more.

All the aforementioned effects are generally and strongly positive, based on an abundance of research

studies from the 1920s to the present. (Phelps, 2005f)

Again, those who claim a paucity of evidence for testing's achievement effects either have not looked very hard, or do not wish to find it.

The vast research literature that is not there

A key component of our faith in progress is the corollary belief that our base of knowledge continually expands. That is, we know what we already know, and we are always learning more. But, the continual expansion of knowledge requires both that the historical accumulation of knowledge be preserved and that new knowledge be welcomed.

Studies measuring benefits from standardized testing with stakes in education date back over a century and range across virtually all relevant types of research methodologies. (Dempster, 1991, 1997) In an appendix of *Defending Standardized Testing* (Phelps, 2005f), I list over 300 different studies, 80 being meta-analyses or reviews of multiple separate studies. Since the publication of that list, I have found hundreds more. Moreover, psychologists have not stopped investigating these issues. (See, for example, Berk, 1999; Bourque, 2005; Cheng & Watanabe, 2004; Dempster, 1997; Driscoll, et al., 2003; Everding, 2006; Hambleton, 2006; Karpicke & Roediger, in press; Leighton, 2007; Marsh, et al., in press; Roediger & Karpicke, 2006a, 2006b.)

Yet, at the same time, the number of researchers asserting the research literature's nonexistence continues to grow. Moreover, the belief seems to have become pervasive, transcending political and ideological boundaries.

One might reasonably assume, given the thrust of U.S. education policy in the early 2000s, that this research literature would have been exposed, made widely familiar, and meticulously analyzed. But, just the opposite happened, for reasons I do not claim to understand. Ironic and, perhaps, inexplicable— the bulk of an available research literature that could have helped to guide our society in the implementa-

tion of its primary, and controversial, education policy, was declared nonexistent.

To my observation, these efforts at information suppression, irrespective of their motivation, have been largely successful. Prominent education researchers have managed to delete large segments of the education research literature from the collective working memory and hide information that could have instructed U.S. education policy makers.

Comprehensive testing systems are multi-leveled and multi-targeted

A comprehensive testing system is one that captures all the benefits standardized testing offers, and does it for all students, not just some. Large-scale, standards-based, high-stakes educational tests offer three benefits:

1. information for diagnosis (e.g., of individual students or teachers, of schools, of school programs);
2. efficiencies from alignment, when the tests are matched to curricular standards and teachers teach to those standards (and, yes, teach "to the test," as they are supposed to do with standards-based tests);
3. motivation to study and to attain goals.

The most efficient testing regimes, such as one finds in many European and Asian countries, tap all three sources of benefits through multi-level and multi-target systems. "Multi-level" means that high-stakes tests are administered at more than just one educational level. Typically in European and Asian systems, students face high-stakes tests at the beginning and/or end of more than one educational level (e.g., at the end of primary school, the beginning and/or end of lower secondary school, the beginning and/or end of upper secondary school, and the beginning and/or end of postsecondary education).

"Multi-target" means that every student, no matter where they are in the range of achievement levels or in their choice of curriculum, faces a high-stakes test that, ideally, offers a challenging, but attainable, goal. In some systems, tests are set at multiple levels of difficulty, and offer multiple levels of certification (e.g., a "regular" diploma and an "honors" diploma). In other systems, different tests cover different subject matter (e.g., general, vocational, and academic; literature, math & science, technology, and social science).

In the United States, tests with high stakes for students are uncommon at any but the upper secondary level (i.e., high school). Moreover, with very few exceptions, they are single-target tests—each and every student, no matter what their level of achievement or ability, course selection, or curricular preference, must meet a single standard of performance.

Ironically, largely socialist Europe, with its relatively small socioeconomic (and academic achievement) disparity, acknowledges that children are different and offers them a range of academic options and multiple achievement targets. In the more libertarian United States, with its relatively large socioeconomic (and academic achievement) disparity, pressure is brought to bear for all children to take the same curriculum (i.e., what is often called the "college track") and a single academic achievement target is set for all.

When only one academic achievement target is offered, by necessity it must be a low target. If it is not, huge numbers of students can fail and the educational system can collapse upon itself. When the single target is low, responsive school systems focus effort and resources toward bringing low-achieving students up to that target. Unfortunately, they also may neglect the average- and higher-achieving students or, in the most perverse cases, deliberately hold them back.

The federal No Child Left Behind (NCLB) Act set in place what is largely a testing program. NCLB, however, falls far short of a comprehensive multi-

level, multi-target high-stakes testing system. State NCLB testing systems typically set only one target (for schools), in only three subjects, no stakes for students (so little motivation to take the test seriously), and curricular alignment can be less than perfect. Yet, as little as it may be, NCLB is commonly characterized by educators and journalists as either being too much or else marking the limit of what our schools can bear.

GLOSSARY

End-of-course test—test administered at the end of a course of study, such as that for algebra I or chemistry.

Item rotation—for tests that are administered periodically, the process of replacing some number of already-used test items with others that have similar content and statistical characteristics.

Lake Wobegon effect—score inflation or artificial test score gains.

Mastery testing—when students are tested periodically for diagnosis as many times as necessary to prove mastery of the material. In mastery learning regimes, each student may progress at a different pace, but ends up in the same place, mastering the material.

Predictive validity—correlation between test scores and future performance.

Score inflation—a rise in test scores over time that is not caused by a genuine increase in the quality being measured, such as academic achievement.

Standards for Educational and Psychological Testing—produced by the APA, NCME, and AERA; have become the de facto regulations governing legal uses and administration of most standardized tests in the United States.

Test score pollution—term coined by Haladyna, Nolen, and Haas (1991), derived from earlier work by Messick (1984), that "refers to factors affecting the truthfulness of a test score interpretation. Specifically, pollution increases or decreases test performance without connection to the construct represented by the test, producing construct-irrelevant test score variance."

Unintended consequences—another way of saying that standardized testing may portend adverse effects (e.g., students who

score poorly might get hurt feelings, or be held back a grade).

Washback effect—when some aspect of a test given at one grade level has an effect on school, teacher, or student behavior in earlier grades (a.k.a. backwash effect).

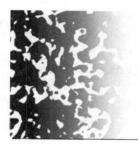

Mechanics of Test Development and Quality Assurance

Validity

the extent to which a test measures the quality it purports to measure; there are several kinds (e.g., content, construct, criterion, consequential, predictive). Unlike reliability, validity can sometimes be difficult to measure precisely.

Content validity

the extent to which the content of a test is representative of the conceptual or content domain it is designed to cover. Content validation is a process used to establish the meaning of a test through a series of studies.

All standardized tests should be valid, reliable, and fair.

Validity refers to the degree to which evidence and theory support the interpretations of test scores, those interpretations being dependent on the proposed uses of the scores. It is the interpretation of the test score and how it is used that is validated, not the test.

Establishing test validity is an ongoing process and entails gathering different kinds of evidence. For example, evidence of **content validity** relies on subject-matter experts to review test items to ensure that items accurately measure the content. The closely related **curricular validity** is strong if a test contains questions based on the content of the curriculum and weak if a test contains questions not based on the content of the curriculum.

Evidence of **criterion validity** relies on the relationship between different test scores that measure the same content. If there is a strong, positive relationship (i.e., correlation) between scores on two

Curricular validity

strong if a test contains questions based on the content of the curriculum and weak if a test contains questions not based on the content of the curriculum.

Criterion validity

the extent to which a test score corresponds to an accurate measure of interest; the measure of interest is called the criterion.

Concurrent validity

a form of criterion validity in which the test and the criterion are administered at the same point in time.

Construct validity

indicates that the test scores are to be interpreted as indicating the test taker's standing on the construct measured by the test.

Construct

the quality or concept a test is designed to measure.

Construct equivalence

the extent to which the construct measured by one test is essentially the same as the construct measured by another test.

Construct irrelevance

the extent to which test scores are influenced by factors unrelated to the test's intended construct.

different tests designed to measure proficiency in Geometry, for example, it is considered one source of evidence that both tests are valid measures of proficiency in Geometry. **Concurrent validity** is a form of criterion validity in which the test and the criterion are administered at the same point in time.

Construct validity indicates that the test scores are to be interpreted as indicating the test taker's standing on the **construct** measured by the test. To evaluate construct validity, a researcher simultaneously defines some construct and develops the instrumentation to measure it. In the studies, observed correlations between the test and other measures come to define the meaning of the test. Scores from two tests are said to be **construct equivalent** when the extent to which the construct measured by one is essentially the same as that measured by the other. Test scores are said to be **construct irrelevant** when they are influenced by factors that are irrelevant to the construct that the test is intended to measure. Such extraneous factors distort the meaning of test scores.

Consequential validity is the correlation between test scores and intended outcomes. For example, if a testing agency asserts that the process of taking a certain test will increase student motivation, evidence for consequential validity could be a study finding that student motivation did, in fact, increase due to test-taking.

Reliability indicates the extent to which scores are consistent across different administrations and/or different scorers. It is the test score that is or is not reliable, not the test. The term is also sometimes used more generally to describe **measurement error**—theoretically the difference in scores from the same test (or parallel forms of the test) that has been given to the same examinee many times. Of course, an examinee typically does not take the same test, or even parallel forms of a test, many times, much less do so independently (i.e., with no memory of previous efforts). So, statisticians have

Consequential validity

correlation between test scores and intended outcomes.

developed methods for estimating measurement error. All tests are subject to measurement error.

Test scores are *fair* when they yield score interpretations that are valid and reliable for all students taking the test, regardless of ethnicity, national origin, gender, or disability. Tests should measure the same knowledge and skills for all who take the test. Test scores should not systematically underestimate or overestimate the knowledge and skills of members of a particular group.

The test development process

Reliability

refers to the degree to which test scores are consistent across time, conditions, and test-takers.

In development, a test is planned, constructed, evaluated, modified, analyzed, and reported. Though the administration of a test and the reporting of results are often considered separate, the test development process does not stop with the first test administration as the resulting data must be analyzed, the passing scores set, and the analysis prepared for reporting.

Measurement error

the component of an observed test score that is not the true score of the quality that you wish to measure.

The process typically includes the following steps. (Please note, however, that different people may use the same terms in different ways. For example, one east coast state identifies as "test blueprint" what its neighboring state calls "test framework," and vice versa.)

Define the character and purpose.

A test is developed for a purpose; the more clearly that purpose can be defined operationally, the smoother the process will be. Most tests are sponsored by a public agency or some other policy-making body. That agency is responsible for clarifying and communicating the nature and purpose of the test, the characteristics of the population to be tested, and the intended uses of test results (e.g., selection to a program, monitoring instruction).

Test specifications

much like the "specs" for a construction or design project. The idea is to set the parameters within which developers will work.

Test specifications. . . . are much like the "specs" for a construction or design project. The idea is to set the parameters within which developers will work—the steps, schedule, production and progress benchmarks, content domains, approximate number

of test items, test format, item formats (e.g., multiple-choice, short answer), the desired statistical properties of test items, and so on. Test specs may be included in the proposal a test developer submits to bid on a test development contract.

Test frameworks. . . . are outlines of test content, detailed enough to be read meaningfully by item writers and providing the information they need to understand the needed character and content for each test item. Particular attention is usually paid to how the items work together as a whole in tapping the relevant content domain (i.e., the "cognitive classification system"). Typically, developers try to include items within each content domain (and sub-domain) that range in difficulty and in cognitive complexity. For the latter task, many psychometricians still use one or another version of the *Taxonomy of Educational Objectives,* developed a half century ago by Benjamin Bloom and colleagues: 1. knowledge; 2. comprehension; 3. application; 4. analysis; 5. synthesis; and 6. evaluation. (Bloom, et al., D., 1956)

Test blueprints. . . . serve much the same purpose as architects' blueprints. They provide more detail than the specs, showing how the different pieces of a test will fit together. The test is divided into its component sections and, for each section, the content is defined, the number and type of test items chosen, and criteria are set by which decisions will be made for keeping or deleting test items after they are reviewed and field tested. Blueprints are given to the statisticians and computer programmers who assemble each test form, choosing items from among those available in the **item pool**.

Test assembly. . . . is the final step before printing test forms. Considerations at this stage include how items should be ordered and grouped, how items will look on a page, how the test should be printed, and how test security should be maintained during storage and shipping.

Test frameworks

outlines of test content, detailed enough to be read meaningfully by item writers.

Test blueprints

serve much the same purpose as architects' blueprints. They provide more detail than the specs, showing how the different pieces of a test will fit together.

Item pool

the population of test items from which a testing organization may choose when assembling a test form.

Develop test items

Test items

consist of questions or prompts designed to elicit an answer or response and, perhaps, a set of possible answers.

Distracters

of the responses a test taker may choose in a selected-response (or, multiple choice) item, the ones that are incorrect.

Selected-response format

requires test taker to select a response to a question or prompt. Types of selected-response items include multiple-choice, true-false, and matching.

Test items should be developed using clearly defined, common sense rules. Selected-response (e.g., multiple choice) items, for example, must be accurate, valid, and clear, with options (i.e., **distracters**) that are plausible to students not well grounded in the subject matter. Constructed-response prompts also must be clear, based on subject matter students have been taught, and be fully answerable within the time frame allotted for the response.

Item writing. Psychometricians themselves write few test items. Most item writers are subject-matter experts, experienced instructors, or both. Here is how one testing firm advertised item writer positions (ACT, Inc., 2007b):

> ACT item writers are educators like you from across the United States. We work with a diverse group of item writers to help ensure that our English, Reading, Mathematics, and Science Tests represent what is being taught in classrooms nationwide and reflect a balance in gender, race/ethnicity, and geographical representation.
>
> - Teachers for grades 4 through 8 can develop test materials for grade-level Science and n Mathematics Tests. Teachers for grade 8 can also develop tests for the EXPLORE program.
> - High school teachers can develop test materials for the EXPLORE, PLAN, and ACT programs.
>
> Postsecondary educators can develop test materials for the ACT program.

Item formats. The **selected-response format** (e.g., multiple-choice) is efficient, practical, and usually produces highly reliable results. It offers the advantages of objectivity and uniformity in scoring, ease of administration, and low cost as, generally, machines can do the scoring. Moreover, students typically can answer them more quickly than constructed-response items (e.g., essays). Thus, in the same amount of testing time, selected-response items can cover a broader range of content domain than can constructed-response items.

Constructed-response item

type of performance item for which the test taker is required to compose a response to a question or prompt. Types of constructed-response items include fill-in-the-blank, short answer, and essay.

Higher-order thinking

a grab-bag of cognitive processes alleged to be related to creativity, such as lateral thinking and meta-analysis. It is sometimes asserted that standardized tests cannot test higher-order thinking. More often, it is asserted that standardized tests with multiple-choice response formats cannot test higher-order thinking (but open-ended response formats can).

Constructed-response items are often included in a test along with multiple-choice items in order to obtain additional and different types of information about what a student knows or can do. The constructed-response format allows a student more flexibility in responding, as selected-response items constrain students to a single appropriate answer. But, scoring constructed-response items can be expensive and time consuming.

Still, many educators believe that, despite their lower reliability and greater cost, constructed-response items allow students to be creative and to demonstrate a more in-depth understanding of content. Selected-response items can do just as well, or even better, at measuring complex reasoning and problem-solving abilities, however, if care is taken in their development. In cognitive laboratories, for example, psychologists break down examinees' responses to selected-response items in great detail, and analyze them. Cognitive labs are much like (and sometimes are) human factors labs, which are probably most well-known for their use in analyzing the human-machine interactions of airplane pilots' instruments. (Powers & Kaufman, 2002)

The Educational Testing Service illustrates how both multiple-choice and constructed-response items can be either simple or complex and require either lower- or **higher-order**, thinking. An ETS brochure provides four examples of a test item written on the same topic: in "factual" multiple-choice, "analytical" multiple-choice, factual constructed-response, and analytical constructed-response formats (ETS Board of Trustees, 1991). I contrast here their examples of the item written in analytical multiple-choice and factual-recall constructed-response format:

Factual-recall constructed-response format:

- What does the Thirteenth Amendment to the U.S. Constitution of the United States prohibit?

Analytical multiple-choice format:

- Which of the following best describes the constitutional interpretation of federation?

(A) The federal government and the states each have separate and mutually exclusive roles and responsibilities; neither controls the other.

(B) The states have some powers reserved to them which they may exercise if the Supreme Court permits.

(C) The federal government and the states have separate but overlapping powers; where these powers conflict, federal powers prevail.

(D) The states may only exercise those power delegated to them by Congress.

(E) The federal government may exercise only those powers specifically enumerated in the Constitution.

In this comparison, at least, the multiple-choice item requires more complex, higher-order thinking than does the constructed-response item.

Other item formats are available for tests without right or wrong answers. The Likert scale, for example, is often used to survey attitudes or preferences. Statements are presented, and respondents indicate the degree to which they agree or disagree, usually on an odd-numbered scale, with the midpoint representing a neutral position. The most common Likert scales are probably one-to-five and one-to-seven. More exotic item formats include the inkblots and other visual images used in **projective tests**.

Test directions

Item writers must also write clear and unambiguous test directions. Good test directions ensure that the items measure examinees' skills and content knowledge. Directions should include practice items, suggestions for allocating time, advice about guessing, and information about test-taking strategies.

Field testing (i.e., pilot testing)

After items are written, they must be evaluated. Item evaluation starts with feedback gathered from pretests conducted internally by the test developer to uncover unclear wording or directions, inappropriate timing, fairness issues, and/or levels of difficulty. Formal **field tests** involve test takers with

---

Projective test

presents an ambiguous stimulus and requests the test taker to describe or explain. The assumption is that people respond by projecting their own inner thoughts, feelings, fears, or conflicts onto the stimuli. The Rorschach Inkblot Test and the Thematic Apperception Test are probably the most famous.

Field test

a practice, not an operational, test involving volunteers with characteristics similar to those of the population that will be tested.

characteristics similar to those of the population that will be tested. They provide more detailed technical data on item quality. Field testing can be accomplished in a stand-alone test administration or by embedding non-scorable new items in a regular, **operational test**.

Item analysis *(i.e., key verification)*

Using data gathered from a test administration, item analysis evaluates their statistical properties, in particular their difficulty, discrimination, and differential functioning (DIF). The most commonly used measure of **item difficulty** is the **p-value**, the simple percentage of test-takers who responded to an item correctly (e.g., a p-value of .75 means that 75% of test-takers responded correctly to an item). Usually, test developers like to have, for each subdomain that may be separately scored, items that range in difficulty.

Items may be compared according to how well they separate those who score high and low on the test. The index of discrimination would then be the correlation between performance on an item and performance on the whole test (e.g., point-biserial correlation). Items that do not discriminate make no statistical contribution to an analysis. A commonly used measure of **item discrimination** is the **point-biserial**, the correlation between test takers' scores on the entire test (or subtest) and their scores on a particular item.

Generally, test takers who do well on a test as a whole are more likely to get any particular item right, and vice versa. Thus, high scorers are more likely to get the difficult items right, and low scorers more likely to get them wrong. Difficult items showing the converse characteristic of low scorers being more likely to get the item correct, may have an underlying flaw (e.g., two possible correct answers) and are usually re-evaluated, and may be removed from the item pool.

Differential item functioning (DIF) is the tendency of an item to function differently with dif-

---

Operational test

a regular, genuine test administration, with the intended test population taking a test "that counts" (i.e., not a field test)

Item analysis

the set of methods used to evaluate test items; the most common techniques involve measurement of item difficulty and discrimination.

Item difficulty

the tendency of an item to receive incorrect responses.

P value

the percentage of test takers who respond with the correct choice.

Item discrimination

refers to how effectively each item differentiates between examinees who know most about the content area being tested and those who know least.

Point-biserial correlation

the correlation between test takers' scores on the whole test and their scores on an item

---

DIF (differential item functioning)

the tendency of an item to show different statistical characteristics with different demographic groups.

ferent groups of test takers, with the groups defined by a background factor not related to proficiency on the test. Test developers worry about high DIF statistics, as that suggests the item is culturally ambiguous. Typically, items identified in a DIF analysis are removed from the item pool, even if the developer cannot figure out why they perform differentially across group.

Item selection

The basic rule for item selection after field testing is to retain items that meet evaluation criteria and have adequate psychometric properties as detailed or defined in the test specifications. Next, they are presented for review by an item review panel.

Expert review

Most standards-based tests are the product of several rounds of review and modification. Typically, a test developer will work with state officials to recruit a representative sample of educators who are expert both in the content and the instruction of the relevant subject matter to serve on review panels. They assemble in one location, sign non-disclosure agreements (some states also require oaths before a notary), and work in jury-like fashion as long as is needed to get the job done.

Framework review

Test frameworks are detailed content outlines, drafted by a test developer. The appropriate reviewers would be educators expert in the content domain. For a chemistry test, for example, high school chemistry teachers and university chemistry professors might be invited.

Item review

After a test framework has been reviewed and modified, items are written to the framework and, then, the items, too, are reviewed. Because the expertise required is the same, in many states, item review panels are staffed by the same folks who worked on framework reviews a few months earlier.

Bias review (i.e., fairness review, sensitivity review)

Bias review panels are quite different. Their task is to remove or revise any draft test items they feel may advantage or disadvantage one or another cultural, gender, or ethnic group. Test items about sports have been cited in the past as examples of possible gender bias. Likewise, items about activities only familiar to wealthier folk have been cited as examples of possible class bias.

It is essential that bias review panels attract a diverse mix of members. Sometimes, only a member of a cultural group can see how an item can be unfair to that group. Bias review is not an exercise in political correctness; it is an essential part of the quality control process.

Passing score review (a.k.a., standard setting)

When a new test is being developed, it is impossible to know exactly how difficult it will be until after an operational test administration. Generally, the first time a new test is administered operationally (i.e., not as a field test), scores are not assigned immediately. Another review panel, perhaps assembled from the group of previous panel members, serves to decide what score should be considered a passing score, if there is to be such a **cut score**, or what scores should be given any other designation.

Cut score

a threshold, a test score that distinguishes between the scores above and below, as does the minimum score required to obtain a diploma.

Test administration and scoring

Test format

refers to the form and content of a test in its administration (e.g., paper-and-pencil, computer-based).

Test format refers to the form and content of a test in its administration. The most common formats are paper-and-pencil and computer-based; other standardized test formats include oral interviews, demonstrations, exhibitions, investigations, and work sample reviews.

Test administration

the act of giving a test.

Because **test administration** environment and procedures can affect performance, great care is usually taken to see that test administration settings vary as little as possible and present the test-taker with no distractions. Test security is of paramount importance, as any breach can compromise the validity of scores.

Accommodations (or, modifications) (e.g., Braille test forms for the blind; a signing test administrator for the deaf) must be made available for those with disabilities, and each accommodation must be appropriate to the disability, as specified in their **Individual Education Plan (IEP).**

In **census testing** everyone in the population of interest is tested. Testing only portions of the population of interest is possible, however, when individual scores are not needed.

Matrix testing

When the purpose of the test is to generate group (i.e., aggregate) scores, each student does not need to be administered all the test items. Instead, each student can be administered a sample of items. Thus, a test consisting of many items can be divided into a number of short tests. Then, each student takes one short test. The population tested can either be a sample or a census depending on the purpose of the test scores. **Matrix testing** does not provide individual scores because students are given too few items to generate a reliable score and it is difficult to create comparability across different forms of the test.

Partial matrix testing

To overcome the limitation in matrix testing (i.e., no individual scores), partial matrix testing offers a compromise. In this design, a set of core items is administered to all students, and other items are matrix sampled across forms. The benefit of this design is that it provides individual scores and more valid and reliable group scores.

Selected sample testing

Once a test population has been defined, a sample of examinees is tested. The sample can be used to generate group level scores. For example, large-scale monitoring tests often test just a small percentage of students in order to calculate a group score.

Score report. . . . usually a computer-generated that provides scores and explanations for the scores

to the test taker, the parents of young students, the student's school, or the organization or institution to which the test taker is applying for admission or employment.

Technical report. . . . a typically very long and legally-important document prepared by test developers and administrators that identifies test development and administration procedures and characteristics in psychometric detail, and reports on all the many relevant statistical analyses involved in test quality control.

Equating. . . . the process of statistically weighting two versions of a test, or two **test forms**, so that equal scores represent equal levels of difficulty. Equating is necessary for maintaining reliable time series such that test scores can be validly compared over time and administrations. Equating requires that different tests or test forms share some test items in common, or in common with a separate **anchor test**.

Test form

a version of a test with a particular combination of items. With large-scale tests, there can be two to many forms developed, for use in the same administration (to prevent answer copying) or in subsequent administrations (to reduce item exposure)

Anchor test

provides information about the equivalence (or not) of two different tests or test forms by measuring more general skills, or something else that is common to both tests. Anchor test data can be used to translate between the other two tests.

A test quality checklist

If a test is of good quality, a test developer, at minimum, should be able to answer, and answer satisfactorily, these questions below:
What is the purpose of the test?

Is there adequate evidence of validity, assuring that test scores are meaningful?

- Is there evidence that the test is accurately measuring the desired knowledge and skills?
- Are the test results valid for the stated purpose and in the particular setting where the test is to be administered?
- Are the test results valid for the specific groups of students taking the test?

Are test scores reliable, with minimal measurement error?

- Are test results consistent across administrations and scorers?

- Is the level of measurement error for the test small enough that any possible misclassification of students would be inconsequential?

Are the conclusions drawn from test scores fair to all students?

- Are the conclusions drawn from the test results accurate for all students?
- Does the evidence indicate that the test is measuring the same content for all students?
- Is there solid evidence that the test results do not systematically underestimate or overestimate the knowledge or skills of members of any particular group?
- Have cut scores been established for performance levels that will provide accurate and meaningful information for all students (for tests with stakes).

Classical test theory & item response theory

True score

in practice, an individual's or group's long-term average score; in theory, the score that would be obtained if measurement error were absent.

Classical test (i.e., true score) theory

developing a test this way, every test is custom-designed and relevant to a particular population.

Item response (i.e., latent trait) theory (IRT)

comparison with classical test theory, IRT offers "item-free test person measurement" and "person-free item measurement."

Standardized tests are developed through a demanding and time-consuming process based on either classical test theory (using a classical **true score** model) or item response theory (using a "latent trait" model).

Typically, all the steps listed above are necessary to develop a test under **classical test theory**, for which every test is custom-designed and relevant to a particular population. First, one develops a test content framework, or outline, and then validates it with reviews by experts, or current job holders. Next, one drafts test items and field tests them with a representative sample of the test-taking population, which can be difficult to do without exposing that population to the test content. The test development process can take from 18 months to three years to complete.

Most tests are still developed under classical test theory methods, and many kinds of tests (e.g., for small groups, for new constructs) may always be. But, the enormous increases in computing power have made it possible to develop many large-scale tests with **item response theory (IRT)** methods.

IRT was the brainchild of the American Frederic M. Lord (and, separately, the Dane Georg Rasch) over half a century ago. But, Lord's theoretical paper lay dormant for decades until computer power matured sufficiently to handle the extra demands of IRT. (communication with Ron Hambleton, September 2006)

IRT

> . . . rests on two basic postulates: (a) The performance of an examinee on a test item can be predicted by a set of factors called traits, latent traits, or abilities; and (b) the relationship between examinees' item performance and the set of traits underlying item performance can be described by a monotonically increasing function called an item characteristic function or item characteristic curve (ICC). This function specifies that as the level of the trait increases, the probability of a correct response to an item increases. (Hambleton, Swaminathan, & Rogers, 1991, 7)

Not all of the development steps listed above are necessary when tests are developed under item response theory—field testing and item analysis, for example. By comparison with classical test theory, IRT offers "item-free person measurement" and "person-free item measurement." IRT places test takers on a single, common proficiency or ability scale (even though the actual items for one content area may be different than the items for another content area).

IRT comes in one- (the **Rasch model**), two-, and three-parameter flavors, the **parameters** being separate characteristics of the logistic function, or **item characteristic curve**:

1. item difficulty, or p-value (mean horizontal value),
2. item discrimination (slope of the function at the mean), and
3. pseudo-chance, or guessing (horizontal base of the function).

IRT permits estimation of item analysis statistics (e.g., difficulty, discrimination, random chance/

Rasch model

a one-parameter IRT model, named for the Danish statistician, Georg Rasch.

Parameter

an item characteristic curve can be identified by one (item difficulty), two (item discrimination), or three (base value for guessing) parameters.

Item characteristic curve

a graph (or function) of a test item with the measured trait/ability/attitude represented by the x axis and the probability of correct responses represented by the y axis.

Standard error

the error of an estimate due to sampling, based on the number of observations and their distances from the mean.

Item exposure

the degree to which test items are publicly revealed; conversely, the number of times a test item has been used in periodical test administrations, risking exposure.

guessing rate) and person parameters (e.g., ability, attitude) that are invariant, at least in theory, to the particular sample of subjects used to compute the parameter estimates. Moreover, IRT provides estimates of **standard errors** for individual ability estimates, rather than a single estimate for the entire population of test takers, as classical test theory does. These advantages allow IRT testing to transcend many of the limitations that bind classical measurement, such as sample dependency, lack of generalizability, and some **item exposure** effects. (Hambleton, Swaminathan, & Rogers, 1991)

But, IRT tests impose other burdens. It can, for instance, be difficult to meet the technical requirements imposed by IRT's underlying assumptions. IRT tests require larger, sometimes much larger, item pools than do classical tests. Likewise, IRT tests require larger, sometimes much larger, examinee populations, depending on the level of precision required. Moreover, most current applications of IRT assume measurement of just one underlying ability/attitude/trait (e.g., mathematics proficiency) at a time.

Some applied psychometricians working in test development complain that IRT is more popular with academic theoreticians than with them. IRT may be theoretically more elegant and, in some respects, better for basic research. But, psychometricians in the field trying to make IRT work in practice can become frustrated when an IRT "black box" mathematical model doesn't quite fit the data halfway through a test development project, or some already-tested items develop bizarre item response statistics in later use. Critics accuse IRT test developers of conveniently relaxing their assumptions when they hit a statistical snag.

Essentially, IRT imposes a mathematical form—a logistic function—on test data whereas, under classical test theory, a function is built up from the data. Stretching a metaphor, one could say that IRT is more a deductive process and classical test theory is more inductive.

Advocates for IRT might take umbrage at the "black box" aspersion, and remind classical test theorists that they take short cuts of their own, for example, with the requirement (and conundrum) of field testing items on the population to be tested. Such is necessary, though literally impossible, in order to learn essential item response characteristics in advance of test assembly. Classical theorists typically end up field testing items on a population *similar* to the one they will test operationally.

Moreover, IRT makes adaptive testing practicable. **Adaptive testing** is an interactive process whereby each test item after the first is chosen for the examinee based on the examinee's responses to the previous items on the same test. Adaptive testing can save time, by not presenting an examinee items unlikely to inform (i.e., statistically discriminate). Some examinees can finish in a fraction of the time of non-adaptive test, particularly those who know all the answers, or none of them.

Adaptive testing

A sequential form of individual testing in which successive items, or sets of items, in the test are chosen based primarily on their psychometric properties and content, in relation to the test taker's responses to previous items.

Computer-based testing

Computer-based testing (CBT) allows for "on demand" testing. An examinee makes an appointment when ready for the test, possibly any day of the week and any time of the year. In some cases, CBTs can provide an examinee with a test score immediately afterwards

Computer-adaptive testing (CAT) owes its existence and its increasing popularity to IRT. With CAT, test-takers are presented an item at a level of difficulty determined by their performance on the previous item. Correct responses yield more difficult subsequent items. Those responding to all items correctly can finish the examination early, by circumventing the need to respond to the less difficult items.

With the adoption of computers for test delivery, the time needed to take an exam was shortened, but some worried that the computer itself might prove a barrier to people unfamiliar with the use of

Computer-based testing (CBT)

any testing administered by computer, with item selection and order determined either serially or by an adaptive (CAT) algorithm.

Computer-adaptive testing (CAT)

test-takers are presented an item at a level of difficulty determined by their performance on the previous item. For example, correct responses may yield more difficult subsequent items, and vice versa.

machines. In addition, the always-available aspect of computer test delivery increased item exposure.

In 1993, ETS introduced a computer-adaptive version of the GRE, which was slated to eventually replace the old paper-and-pencil version of the test, at 170 testing centers nationwide. The next year, ETS discovered that employees of a test preparation course were taking the test, memorizing as much of it as they could, and then recreating a large portion of the exam after the fact (an activity that has since come to be known as "braindumping"). With test security compromised, ETS suspended administration of the computerized test for a week in December 1994 while tightening various security protocols.

To make braindumping more difficult, ETS reduced the number of times the GRE would be offered by computer. ETS also filed suit against Kaplan Educational Centers, the largest of the test preparation companies, alleging copyright infringement and seeking a court order forbidding its employees from retaking the test.

Test development standards and guidelines

According to Holmen and Docter (1972, 34), standards and guidelines for standardized test development and administration began with the establishment of a test service department at the World Book Company in the early 1920s. The Test Department published popular bulletins that "provided simple, nontechnical discussions of test topics and practical examples of effective uses of tests. In addition, World sponsored an early series of books on measurement theory and practice."

Through the 1920s, however, the responsibility for the integrity of each standardized test rested with the test author. With the establishment of its Division of Test Research and Service in the 1930s, World Book began to manage some links in the value chain itself, such as the "development and standardization of tests, which were beyond the resources of individual authors or groups of authors" (Holmen & Docter, 1972, 34). The company became a partner

in test development, with test authors bringing subject-matter and psychological expertise and World Book providing the technical and experimental facilities.

The World Book Company's renowned efforts to standardize the standardized test development process formed the basis for some of the sections of the original Standards for Educational and Psychological Tests and Manuals which, in turn, became the forerunner of today's industry bible, the **Standards for Educational and Psychological Testing** (Ekstrom, Elmore, & Schafer, 1997). As mentioned earlier, the Standards are not laws or regulations, but have been treated by the courts as if they were (Buckendahl & Hunt, 2005; Phillips, 1996, 2000).

Standardized tests are now developed through a demanding and time-consuming process according to detailed and rigorous technical standards that have, for all practical purposes, become legally required (see, for example, Buckendahl & Hunt, 2005; Plake, 2005; Geisinger, 2005; O'Boyle & McDaniel, 2007). Some critics of standardized testing seem to be unaware of both the extent of the technical safeguards and the imperative for test developers to follow them. Indeed, some persistent criticisms were answered by psychometricians long ago, and written into one or more set of technical standards which have, in turn, been followed scrupulously by test developers for years.

This is not to say that test developers do not sometimes make mistakes—we all do—or sometimes try to cut corners too sharply under budget pressure. But, as some of the accusations proffered by critics, and accepted unreservedly by journalists, become over time more outdated and far-fetched, the potential demands on the test development process become more unreasonable.

Technical standards for test development and administration have been composed or endorsed by dozens of professional organizations (see below). The various standards documents continue to be revised and updated, as needed. Putting all of them

together would construct a pile thousands of pages high.

Listed here are citations for some of the many such documents produced by North American or international organizations. Governments and professional organizations outside North America have produced many more (see, for example, Leach & Oakland).

SELECTED TESTING STANDARDS AND GUIDELINES

American Counseling Association & Association for Assessment in Counseling. (2003). *Responsibilities of users of standardized tests* (3rd edition) (RUST).

American Educational Research Association (AERA), American Psychological Association (APA), & National Council on Measurement in Education (NCME). (1999). *Standards for educational and psychological testing.* Washington, DC: Authors.

American Federation of Teachers, National Council on Measurement in Education, & National Education Association. (1990). *Standards for teacher competence in educational assessment of students.* Washington, DC: Author.

American Psychological Association. (1992). *Ethical principles of psychologists and code of conduct.* Washington, DC: Author.

American Psychological Association. (1998, August). *Testing and assessment: Rights and responsibilities of test takers: Guidelines and expectations.* Washington, DC: Author.

American Psychological Association, Practice and Science Directorates. (2000). *Report of the task force on test user qualifications.* Washington, DC: Author.

American Psychological Association. (2001, May). *Appropriate use of high-stakes testing in our nation's schools.* Washington, DC: Author.

Association for Assessment in Counseling and Education. (2002, November). *Standards for educational and psychological testing—What counselors need to know.* Alexandria, VA: Author.

Association for Assessment in Counseling. (2003). *Standards for multicultural assessment.* Alexandria, VA: Author.

Association of Test Publishers. (2002). *Guidelines for computer-based testing.* Washington, DC: Author.

Association of Test Publishers. (n.d.). *Model guidelines for pre-employment integrity testing.* Washington, DC: Author.

International Personnel Management Association—Assessment Council (IPMAAC). (2004, June). *Policies and procedures manual.*

International Test Commission. (1999). *International guidelines for test use.* Louvain-la-Neuve, Belgium: Author.

International Test Commission. (2006). *Guidelines on adapting tests.* http://www.intestcom.org/itc_projects.htm

International Test Commission. (2006). *Guidelines on test use.* http://www.intestcom.org/itc_projects.htm

International Test Commission. (2005). *International guidelines on computer-based and internet-delivered testing.* http://www.intestcom.org/itc_projects.htm

Joint Advisory Committee. (1993). *Principles for fair assessment practices for education in Canada.* Edmonton, Alberta: Author.

Joint Committee on Standards for Educational Evaluation. (2007). *The personnel evaluation standards.* Kalamazoo, MI: Western Michigan University, Evaluation Center.

Joint Committee on Standards for Educational Evaluation. (2007). *The program evaluation standards 2.* Kalamazoo, MI: Western Michigan University, Evaluation Center.

Joint Committee on Standards for Educational Evaluation. (2007). *The student evaluation standards.* Kalamazoo, MI: Western Michigan University, Evaluation Center.

Joint Committee on Testing Practices. (2005). *Code of fair testing practices in education.* Washington, DC: Author.

Leach, M. M. & Oakland, T. (2007). Ethics standards impacting test development and use: A review of 31 ethics codes impacting practices in 35 countries. *International Journal of Testing. 7(1),* 71–88.

National Association of College Admission Counselors. (1988). *Statement of principles of good practice.* Alexandria, VA: Author.

National Association of College Admission Counselors. (1995). *Recommendations of the Commission on the Role of Standardized Testing in College Admission Testing.* http://www.nacacnet.org/NR/rdonlyres/50FB8D74–5C89–4996–896A-08476ABA0B72/0/RcmdCmmsnRoleStndTstColAdmNEW.pdf

National Commission for Certifying Agencies. (2004). *Standards for the accreditation of certification programs.* Washington, DC: National Organization for Competency Assurance.

NCME Ad Hoc Committee on the Development of a Code of Ethics. (1995). *Code of professional responsibilities in educational measurement.* Washington, DC: National Council on Measurement in Education.

Nester, M.A., Bruyere, S., & Wall, J. (2003). *Pre-employment testing and the ADA.* Alexandria, VA: Association for Assessment in Counseling and Education, Cornell, American Rehabilitation Counseling Association.

Plake, B. S. & Jones, P. (2002, February). Ensuring fair testing practices: The responsibilities of test sponsors, test developers, test administrators, and test takers in ensuring fair testing practices. Paper presented at the 2002 meeting of the Association of Test Publishers, Carlsbad, CA.

Rights and responsibilities of test takers: Guidelines and expectations. (2002). *ASHA Desk Reference, 1*, 305–311.

Society of Industrial and Organizational Psychology, Inc. (2003). *Principles for the validation and use of personnel selection procedures (4th ed.).* Bowling Green, OH: Author.

U.S. Department of Labor & U.S. Department of Justice, Civil Service Commission, Equal Employment Opportunity Commission. (1978). Uniform guidelines on employee selection procedures. *Federal Register, 43(166),* 38290–39315.

GLOSSARY

Accommodation—a modification of test administration format and procedure devised to accommodate students with disabilities that render them unable to take a test fairly under standard format and procedure.

Adaptive testing—A sequential form of individual testing in which successive items, or sets of items, in the test are chosen based primarily on their psychometric properties and content, in relation to the test taker's responses to previous items.

Anchor test—provides information about the equivalence (or not) of two different tests or test forms by measuring more general skills, or something else that is common to both tests. Anchor test data can be used to translate between the other two tests.

Census testing—every student in the population is tested (unless there are handicapping conditions that make testing impossible for some students).

Classical test (i.e., true score) theory—developing a test this way, every test is custom-designed and relevant to a particular population.

Computer-adaptive testing (CAT)—test-takers are presented an item at a level of difficulty determined by their performance on the previous item. For example, correct responses may yield more difficult subsequent items, and *vice versa.*

Computer-based testing (CBT)—any testing administered by computer, with item selection and order determined either serially or by an adaptive (CAT) algorithm.

Concurrent validity—a form of criterion validity in which the test and the criterion are administered at the same point in time.

Consequential validity—correlation between test scores and intended outcomes.

Construct equivalence—the extent to which the construct measured by one test is essentially the same as the construct measured by another test.

Construct irrelevance—the extent to which test scores are influenced by factors unrelated to the test's intended construct.

Construct validity—indicates that the test scores are to be interpreted as indicating the test taker's standing on the construct measured by the test.

Constructed-response item—type of performance item for which the test taker is required to compose a response to a question or prompt. Types of constructed-response items include fill-in-the-blank, short answer, and essay.

Construct—the quality or concept a test is designed to measure.

Content validity—the extent to which the content of a test is representative of the conceptual or content domain it is designed to cover. Content validation is a process used to establish the meaning of a test through a series of studies.

Criterion validity—the extent to which a test score corresponds to an accurate measure of interest; the measure of interest is called the criterion.

Curricular validity—is strong if a test contains questions based on the content of the curriculum and weak if a test contains questions not based on the content of the curriculum.

Cut score—a threshold, a test score that distinguishes between the scores above and below, as does the minimum score required to obtain a diploma.

DIF (differential item functioning)—the tendency of an item to show different statistical characteristics with different demographic groups.

Distracters—of the responses a test taker may choose in a selected-response (or, multiple choice) item, the ones that are incorrect.

Equating—the process of statistically weighting two versions of a test, or two test forms, so that they are equal in difficulty.

Field test—a practice, not an operational, test involving volunteers with characteristics similar to those of the population that will be tested.

Higher-order thinking—a grab-bag of cognitive processes alleged to be related to creativity, such as lateral thinking and meta-analysis. It is sometimes asserted that standardized tests cannot test higher-order thinking. More often, it is asserted that standardized tests with multiple-choice response formats

cannot test higher-order thinking (but open-ended response formats can).

Individual Education Plan (IEP)—schools must devise an academic program uniquely appropriate to each student who has been identified with a disability that impedes learning.

Item analysis—the set of methods used to evaluate test items; the most common techniques involve measurement of item difficulty and discrimination.

Item characteristic curve—a graph (or function) of a test item with the measured trait/ability/attitude represented by the *x* axis and the probability of correct responses represented by the *y* axis.

Item difficulty—the tendency of an item to receive incorrect responses.

Item discrimination—refers to how effectively each item differentiates between examinees who know most about the content area being tested and those who know least.

Item exposure—the degree to which test items are publicly revealed; conversely, the number of times a test item has been used in periodical test administrations, risking exposure.

Item pool—the population of test items from which a testing organization may choose when assembling a test form.

Item response (i.e., latent trait) theory (IRT)—By comparison with classical test theory, IRT offers "item-free test person measurement" and "person-free item measurement."

Matrix testing—a test consisting of many items is divided into a number of short tests. Each student takes one short test. Student performance on each of the short tests is aggregated to produce a group level score (e.g., school score, state score).

Measurement error—the component of an observed test score that is not the true score of the quality that one wishes to measure.

Operational test—a regular, genuine test administration, with the intended test population taking a test "that counts" (i.e., not a field test).

P value—the percentage of test takers who respond with the correct choice.

Parameter—an item characteristic curve can be identified by one (item difficulty), two (item discrimination), or three (base value for guessing) parameters.

Point-biserial correlation—the correlation between test takers' scores on the whole test and their scores on an item.

Projective test—presents an ambiguous stimulus and requests the test taker to describe or explain. The assumption is that people respond by projecting their own inner thoughts, feelings, fears, or conflicts onto the stimuli. The Rorschach Inkblot Test and the Thematic Apperception Test are probably the most famous.

Rasch model—a one-parameter IRT model, named for the Danish statistician, Georg Rasch.

Reliability—refers to the degree to which test scores are consistent across time, conditions, and test-takers.

Selected-response format—requires a test taker to select a response to a question or prompt. Types of selected-response items include multiple-choice, true-false, and matching.

Standard error—the error of an estimate due to sampling, based on the number of observations and their distances from the mean.

Test administration—the act of giving a test.

Test blueprints—serve much the same purpose as architects' blueprints. They provide more detail than the specs, showing how the different pieces of a test will fit together.

Test form—a version of a test with a particular combination of items. With large-scale tests, there can be two to many forms developed, for use in the same administration (to prevent answer copying) or in subsequent administrations (to reduce item exposure).

Test format—refers to the form and content of a test in its administration (e.g., paper-and-pencil, computer-based).

Test frameworks—are outlines of test content, detailed enough to be read meaningfully by item writers.

Test items—consist of questions or prompts designed to elicit an answer or response and, perhaps, a set of possible answers.

Test specifications—are much like the "specs" for a construction or design project. The idea is to set the parameters within which developers will work.

True score—in practice, an individual's or group's long-term average score; in theory, the score that would be obtained if measurement error were absent.

Validity—the extent to which a test measures the quality it purports to measure; there are several kinds (e.g., content, construct, criterion, consequential, predictive). Unlike reliability, validity can sometimes be difficult to measure precisely.

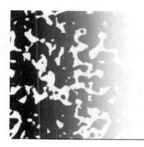

Conclusion

The fact that tests and test results can be misused is beyond dispute. Human beings are responsible for administering them and interpreting their results, and humans are imperfect creatures. There is also no denying that tests are imperfect measurement devices. But some of the alleged problems—that they hurt learning and are expensive, for instance— are disputed by the evidence. Other problems apply equally to the alternatives to testing. Still others are solvable and are being or have been solved by state, local, or national testing directors.

They can, for example, deploy a number of relatively simple solutions to the problems of score inflation, curriculum narrowing, and teaching to the test, including not revealing the contents of tests beforehand; not using the same test twice; adding items on the test that sample broadly from the whole domain of the curriculum tested; requiring that non-tested subjects also get taught (or testing them, too); and maintaining strict precautions against cheating during test administrations.

While it is unfair to test what has not been taught, no such claim can be made about testing what has been taught. When the content domain of a test is the legally-mandated curriculum, attacks of "teaching to the test" can seem silly, since teachers are not only teaching what they should be teaching, they are teaching what they are legally and ethically obligated to teach.

Another argument against testing—that using test results to evaluate schools leads to unfair comparisons between rich districts with highly educated parents and poor districts with less-well educated parents—can be addressed with at least two solutions. The first is to set targets for schools based on their own past performance. The second is to calculate "value added" test scores, or **gain scores**. This method estimates how much value a school adds to the level of achievement that would have been predicted (given the background and prior attainment of students), and then adjusts a school's or district's test scores accordingly. Like any other system, "value-added" scoring can be abused and the scores can also be tricky to calculate and interpret. But, able and earnest analysts are striving to make value-added systems work.

Gain score

the difference between a test taker's score, or a cohort's average score, from one test administration and another, later administration of the same test.

Are the alternatives better?

While some of the problems with standardized testing turn out not to be problems, and others turn out to be solvable, a third set of problems is inherent and inevitable—but similar to those that also afflict the alternatives.

Social promotion

Unfortunately, one common alternative is a system of social promotion with many levels of (nominally) the same subject matter being taught, ranging from classes for self-motivated kids to those for youngsters who quit trying years before, and whom the system has ignored ever since. Those who suffer the most in aimless school programs that lack standards, clear academic goals, and measurement

of progress toward those goals may well be the students themselves. They can be told for 12 years that everything is fine and then graduate uneducated and unskilled.

In the days before statewide testing in North Carolina, according to Jeff Moss, the Associate School Superintendent for the Hoke County schools:

> We had seven levels of instruction for a subject matter, such as seven levels of biology, seven levels of English One, which ranged from remedial to honors or college preparatory. So the teacher expectation was such that if I labeled you a basic student I needed to put you in basic English and not require much from you. (Molpus, 1998)

After the implementation of a testing program, the North Carolina Education Department began to rate schools based on their average test results. But poorly performing schools were neither punished nor abandoned. The department assembled small teams of curriculum and instruction experts to work with those schools for an entire year. The teams helped school staff align their curricula with state academic standards, demonstrated effective teaching techniques, and located additional resources for the schools. In Hoke County, the poorest in the state, students who failed a test were offered after-school classes and then allowed to retake the test without penalty (Molpus, 1998).

A Southern Regional Education Board study (1998) of the Hoke County Schools' reform program found that

> [T]he percentage of students who now meet the state's algebra proficiency standard has doubled. Twenty percent more now meet the history standard. And the high school's overall Scholastic Assessment Test (SAT) scores are up 11 percent over three years. Also employers are more welcoming of graduates now.

The whole process of reform in Hoke County was set in motion by its initial poor showing in the state testing program, which identified the district's academic problems.

The teacher's burden

In the 1910s, researchers Starch and Elliott made copies of two actual English examination papers and sent them to teachers to grade and return. The marks ranged from 50 to 98 percent. One paper, graded by 142 teachers, received fourteen marks below 80 percent and fourteen above 94 percent. "That is, a paper which was considered too poor for a passing grade by some teachers was rated as excellent by others."

Starch and Elliot repeated the procedure with duplicate geometry tests. Teachers' marks on the 116 returned papers ranged from 28 to 92 percent, with twenty grades below 60 percent and nine of 85 percent and above. According to Lincoln and Workman (1936, 7):

> This type of experiment has been repeated many times by investigators and always with similar results. Therefore there is abundant evidence that teachers' marks are a very unreliable means of measurement.

Without high-stakes standardized testing, we would increase our reliance on teacher grading and testing. Are teacher evaluations free of standardized testing's alleged failings? No. Individual teachers can narrow the curriculum to that which they prefer. Grades are susceptible to inflation with ordinary teachers, as students get to know a teacher better and learn his idiosyncrasies. A teacher's (or school's) grades and test scores are far more likely to be idiosyncratic and non-generalizable than any standardized tests.' (Brookhart, 1993; Frary, Cross, & Weber, 1993; Gullickson & Ellwein, 1985; Hills, 1991; Impara & Plake, 1996; McMillan, 2001; Starch & Elliot, 1912, 1913a, 1913b; Stiggins & Conklin, 1992; Stiggins, Frisbee, & Griswold, 1989; Stone, 1995; Stricherz, 2001; Woodruff & Ziomek, 2004a, 2004b)

According to the research on the topic, many teachers consider "nearly everything" when assigning marks, including student class participation, perceived effort, progress over the period of the

course, and comportment, according to one researcher. Actual achievement vis-à-vis the subject matter is just one factor. Indeed, many teachers express a clear preference for non-cognitive outcomes such as "group interaction, effort, and participation" as more important than averaging tests and quiz scores (Cizek, 1996). It's not so much what you know; it's how you act in class. Being enthusiastic and group-oriented gets you into the audience for TV game shows and, apparently, also gets you better grades in school.

One study of teacher grading practices discovered that 66 percent of teachers feel that their perception of a student's ability should be taken into consideration in awarding the final grade (Frary, 1998). Parents of students who assume that their children's grades represent subject matter mastery might well be surprised.

Ownership of the means of instruction

Perhaps it is appropriate to end with first principles.

The U.S. Constitution grants (by deference) responsibility for education to our country's original founding entities, the states, and not to local districts nor to education professionals. State executives and legislators have the legal right and, some would say, the legal obligation, to determine education policy. By implementing high-stakes testing programs, state officials are being responsive to their constituents, who strongly favor such programs.

Hundreds of studies over the past several decades have demonstrated that students in courses with clear and measured goals learn more than students without. And students, and their former-student parents, seem to be fully aware of this. Given the choice in surveys between standards and tests and the lethargy and aimlessness of school without them, most students choose the former. It is only education professionals who oppose them.

Sure, high-stakes tests can be stressful. But, a completely stress-less life is a pretty dull life. Student surveys for decades have revealed little to no evi-

dence of student stress (from academics, anyway) (Phelps, 1998; Yazzie-Mintz, 2007). Indeed, boredom and a lack of challenge have been more frequent complaints. Moreover, the high-stakes tests we give in North America tend to be low level, so low that virtually any student who makes an effort to pass can eventually pass (see, for example, Mass Insight).

By contrast, high-stakes tests in most other industrialized countries are more challenging and more numerous. Most of those testing programs have been in place for many years, students take them in stride, and educators not only support them, many are integrally involved in constructing them. (Eckstein & Noah; Zeng)

Democracy is messy and the people do not always think what one might wish them to think. But, unless and until one endeavors to amend the U.S. Constitution to favor some other system of government, we have the system we have, and denying that is foolish.

As one education professor who clearly dislikes the character of current testing programs puts it (Covaleskie, 2002):

> Educators and their allies are losing the political battles around testing by opposing the current tests without offering realistic ways to allow the larger society and our respective communities to hold us accountable for the effects of our efforts. This makes no sense politically, but, more than that, it is a violation of our responsibilities to democratic governance and a betrayal of the democratic mission of our public schools.

Standardized testing is a part and a product of modern society and its technical advances, population growth, and social problems. Tests have demonstrated utility in meeting some of its challenges; if they had not, they would not be used. Indeed, the persistent opposition to testing from some quarters has forced test developers to operate in an environment of constant scrutiny.

As the U.K.'s Campaign for Real Education (2003) puts it, "Standardized tests . . . are essential

for accountability. They may not be perfect, but they're all we've got."

GLOSSARY

Gain score—the difference between a test taker's score, or a cohort's average score, from one test administration and another, later administration of the same test.

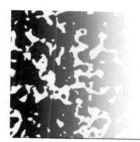

References and Resources

Other primers (and some reference books) on assessment

Association of American Publishers, *Standardized assessment: A primer* http://publishers.org/SchoolDiv/research/research_01/TestingPrimerRevised.pdf http://TestingFACTS.org

American Psychological Association. (2005). *Finding information about psychological tests.* http://www.apa.org/science/faq-findtests.html

Association of Test Publishers. (n.d.). *Answers to questions about tests.* Washington, DC: Author.

Britton, E. D., & Raizen, S. A., (1996). *Examining the examinations: An international comparison of science and mathematics examinations for college-bound students.* Boston: Kluwer Academic.

Center for Academic Integrity. *Academic integrity assessment guide.* http://www.academicintegrity.org/assessGuide.asp

Crocker, L., & Algina, J. (1986). *Introduction to classical and modern test theory.* New York: Harcourt Brace.

CTB/McGraw-Hill: *Accountability and educational progress* http://www.ctb.com/media/articles/pdfs/general/ctb_esea_primer.pdf Other CTB McGraw/Hill Publications include:
- *Beyond the numbers: A guide to interpreting and using the results of standardized achievement tests*
- *A brief guide to test quality*

- *Education assessment: A primer for school boards*
- *A guide for effective assessment*
- *A home guide to understanding tests (in English or Spanish)*
- *Including parents in the teaching and learning process*
- *Inform: A series of special reports*
- *Special accommodations: Meeting the testing needs of students with disabilities*

Dillon, R. F. (1997). *Handbook on testing.* Westport, CT: Greenwood Press.

Downing, S. M. & Haladyna, T. M. (2006). *Handbook of test development.* Mahwah, NJ: Lawrence Erlbaum.

Educational Testing Service, *Using assessments and accountability to raise student achievement.* http://www.ets.org/edreform.html

Educational Testing Service. (2004). *Validity for licensing tests. Teacher Quality Series.* Princeton, NJ: Author.

Giordano, G. (2005). *How testing came to dominate American schools: The history of educational assessment.* New York: Peter Lang.

Haladyna, T. M. (1999). *Developing and validating multiple-choice test items.* Mahwah, NJ: Lawrence Erlbaum.

Hambleton, R. K., Swaminathan, H., & Rogers, H. J. (1991). *Fundamentals of item response theory.* Newbury Park, CA: Sage Publications.

Harcourt Assessment, *Accountability and educational progress.* http://harcourtassessment.com/NR/rdonlyres/320287BB-1F8B-4EE1-B24E-A261C664F18C/0/Accountability_and_Ed_ProgressFinal.pdf. Other Harcourt Educational Measurement publications include: *A checklist for reviewing standardized tests: code of fair testing practices in education; Frequently asked questions; Instructional materials and support; Glossary of measurement terms; Some things parents should know about testing; Tips for taking tests*

Jacoby, R. & Glauberman, N. (1995). *The Bell Curve debate: History, documents, opinions.* New York: Times Books.

Leithwood, K., Edge, K., & Jantzi, D. (1999). *Educational accountability: The state of the art.* International Network for Innovative School Systems (INIS), Gütersloh: Bertelsmann Foundation Publishers.

McKnight, C. C., Crosswhite, F. J., Dossey, J. A., Kifer, E. A., Swafford, J. O., Travers, K. J. & Cooney, T. J. . (1987). *The underachieving curriculum: Assessing U.S. school mathematics from an international perspective.* Champaign, IL: Stipes.

Medrich, E. A., Kagehiro, S. & Houser, J. (1994). *Vocational education in G-7 countries: Profiles and data.* Washington, DC: U.S. Education Department, National Center for Education Statistics.

Moskowitz, J. H. & Stephens, M., Eds. (2004). *Comparing learning outcomes: International assessments and education policy.* London: Routledge.

National Association of State Boards of Education, *A primer on state accountability and large-scale assessments* http://www.nasbe.org/Educational_Issues/Reports/Assessment.pdf

National Organization for Competency Assurance. *Guides to understanding credentialing.* http://www.noca.org/publications/publications.htm

National Organization for Competency Assurance. (2006). *The NOCA guide to understanding credentialing concepts.* Washington, DC. http://www.noca.org/members/CredentialingConcepts.pdf

Occupational Information Network (o*net) Resource Center. (2007). *Testing and Assessment Consumer Guides.* http://www.onetcenter.org/guides.html

Postlethwaite, T. N., Ed. (1996). *International encyclopedia of national systems of education,* Second edition. Oxford: Pergamon.

Robitaille, D. F., Ed. (1997). *National contexts for mathematics and science education: An encyclopedia of the education systems participating in TIMSS.* Vancouver, Canada: Pacific Educational Press.

Scholastic Testing Service. *Local or national norms for achievement tests*

Scholastic Testing Service. *Major misconceptions about "grade equivalent" scores*

Snyderman, M. & Rothman, S. (1990). *The IQ controversy: The media and public policy.* New Brunswick, NJ: Transaction.

Stevenson, H., & Lee, S. (1997). *International comparisons of entrance and exit examinations.* Washington, DC: Office of Educational Research and Improvement, U.S. Department of Education.

Wrightslaw. *Tests and measurements for the parent, teacher, advocate & attorney.* http://www.wrightslaw.com/advoc/articles/tests_measurements.html

Wrightslaw. *Testing: Myths & realities.* http://www.wrightslaw.com/info/test.myths.reality.htm

Zwick, R. (2002). *Fair game? The use of standardized admissions tests in higher education.* New York: RoutledgeFalmer.

References and other print resources

ACT, Inc. (2007a). History of ACT. Retrieved June 25, 2007 from < http://www.act.org/aboutact/history.html >

ACT, Inc. (2007b). Who are ACT item writers? Retrieved June 24, 2007 from < http://www.act.org/humanresources/item/who.html >

America 2000: An education strategy. (1991, April 18). Washington, DC: The White House.

American Educational Research Association, American Psychological Association, & National Council on Measurement in Education. (1999). *Standards for educational and psychological testing.* Washington, DC.

American Federation of Teachers. (1995a). *Defining world class standards.* Washington, D.C.: Author.

American Federation of Teachers. (1995b). *Making standards matter: A fifty-state progress report on efforts to raise academic standards.* Washington, DC: Author.

American Federation of Teachers. (2006, July) Smart testing: Let's get it right: How assessment-savvy have states become since NCLB? *Policy Brief, 19,* Washington, DC: Author.

Averch, H. A., Carroll, Donaldson, Kiesling, & Pincus. (1971). *How effective is schooling? A critical review and synthesis of research findings.* Washington, D.C.: Educational Resources Information Center.

Baker, E. L. (2000). Understanding educational quality: Where validity meets technology. *William H. Angoff Memorial Lecture.* Educational Testing Service, Policy Information Center, Princeton, NJ.

Bangert-Drowns, R. L., Kulik, J. A., & Kulik, C-L. C. (1991, November/December). Effects of frequent classroom testing, *Journal of Educational Research, 85(2),* 89–99.

Barth, P. (2006, April 9). High stakes testing and instruction. National School Board Association, Center for Public Education. Retrieved January 9, 2007, from <http://www.centerforpubliceducation. org/atf/cf/%7B13A13846–1CA6–4F8A-B52E-2A88576B84EF%7D/ HIGH-STAKES_TESTING_04092006.pdf>.

Beaton, A. E. (1996). *Mathematics achievement in the middle school years: IEA's Third International Mathematics and Science Study.* Chestnut Hill, MA: Boston College.

Becker, B. J. (1990). Coaching for the Scholastic Aptitude Test: Further synthesis and appraisal, *Review of Educational Research, 60(3),* Fall, 373–417.

Berk, R. A. (1999). Impact of college admissions and teacher licensure and certification tests on teacher quality, *Impact of Tests on Teacher Quality,* (pp. 217–225). Amherst, MA: National Evaluation Systems.

Bishop, J. H. (1997). *Do curriculum-based external exit exam systems enhance student achievement?* (Paper 97–28). Ithaca, NY: Cornell University, Institute for Labor Relations, Center for Advanced Human Resource Studies.

Bloom, B. S., Ed. & Engelhart, M. D, Hill, W. H., Furst, E. J., & Krathwohl, D. R., (1956). *Taxonomy of educational objectives: The classification of educational goals: Handbook I: Cognitive domain.* New York, NY: David McKay.

Blum, J., (2002, June 9). Grade changes found at top D.C. school: Teacher's discoveries at Wilson High prompt investigation, *Washington Post.* C01.

Bourque, M. L. (2005). Leave no standardized test behind. In R. P. Phelps (Ed.), *Defending standardized testing* (pp. 227–254). Mahwah, NJ: Lawrence Erlbaum.

Bracey, G. (1998). *Put to the test: The omnipresence of tests and what you need to know about them.* Bloomington, IN: Phi Delta Kappa.

Bridgeman, B., McCamley-Jenkins, L., & Ervin, N. (2000). *Prediction of freshman grade-point average from the revised and recentered SAT*

I: Reasoning Test, College Board Report 2000–1. New York, NY: College Board.

Briggs, D.C. (2001, Winter). The effect of admissions test preparation. *Chance.*

Britton, E. D., & Raizen, S. A. (1996*). Examining the examinations: An international comparison of science and mathematics examinations for college-bound students.* Boston, MA: Kluwer Academic.

Britton, E. D., Hawkins, S., & Gandal, M. (1996). Comparing examinations systems. In E.D. Britton & S.A. Raizen (Eds.), *Examining the examinations: An international comparison of Science and Mathematics examinations for college-bound students* (pp. 201–218). Boston, MA: Kluwer Academic.

Brookhart, S. M. (1993, Summer). Teachers' grading practices: Meaning and values, *Journal of Educational Measurement, 30(2).*

Brubacher, J. S. (1966). *A history of the problems of education,* (2nd edition). New York, NY: McGraw-Hill.

Buckendahl, C. W., & Hunt, R. (2005). Whose rules? The relation between the "rules" and "law" of testing. In R. P. Phelps (Ed.), *Defending standardized testing* (pp. 147–158). Mahwah, NJ: Lawrence Erlbaum.

Butts, R. F. (1947). *A cultural history of education.* New York, NY: McGraw-Hill.

Camara, W. (1999, Fall). Is commercial coaching for the SAT I worth the money? *College Counseling Connections 1(1).* New York, NY: The College Board.

Camara, W. (2007). College admission testing: Myths and realities. In R. P. Phelps (Ed.), *The anti-testing fallacies.* Washington, DC: American Psychological Association.

Cameron J. & Pierce, W. D. (1994, Fall). Reinforcement, reward, and intrinsic and extrinsic motivation: A meta-analysis. *Review of Educational Research, 64(3),* 363–423.

Cameron, J. & Pierce, W. D. (1996, Spring). The debate about rewards and intrinsic motivation: Protests and accusations do not alter the results. *Review of Educational Research. 66(1),* 39–51.

Campaign for Real Education (2003, Winter). *Newsletter, 51,* York, U.K.

Cannell, J. J. (1987). *Nationally normed elementary achievement testing in America's public schools: How all fifty states are above the national average.* (2nd Ed.), Daniels, WV: Friends for Education.

Cannell, J. J. (1989). *How public educators cheat on standardized achievement tests.* Albuquerque, NM: Friends for Education.

Carlson, J. F. & Geisinger, K. F. (2007). Psychological diagnostic testing. In R. P. Phelps, (Ed.), *The anti-testing fallacies.* Washington, DC: American Psychological Association.

Carroll, J. B. (1955). The Harvard Foreign Language Aptitude Tests, In the *12th Yearbook of the National Council on Measurements Used in Education, Part 2.* Cleveland.

Cheng, L., & Watanabe, Y. (2004). *Washback in language testing: Research contexts and methods.* Mahwah, NJ: Lawrence Erlbaum.

Cizek, G. J. (1996, December). Grades: The final frontier in assessment reform, *NASSP Bulletin.*

Cizek, G. J. (2001, September). More unintended consequences of high-stakes testing? *Educational Measurement: Issues and Practice,* 1–3, 7.

Clark, D. L., Lotto, L. S. & Astuto, T. A. (1984, Summer). Effective schools and school improvement: A comparative analysis of two lines of inquiry, *Educational Administration Quarterly. 20*(3), 41–68.

Cole, N. & Willingham, W., (1997). *Gender and fair assessment.* Princeton, NJ: ETS.

Cotton, K. (1995). *Effective schooling practices: A research synthesis,* 1995 update, Portland, OR: Northwest Regional Education Laboratory.

Covaleskie, J. F. (2002). Two cheers for standardized testing, *International Electronic Journal for Leadership in Learning. 6(2).* Retrieved May 26, 2007 from <http://www.ucalgary.ca/~iejll/volume6/cova-leskie.html>.

Crocker, L. (2005). Teaching for the test: How and why test preparation is appropriate. In R. P. Phelps (Ed.), *Defending Standardized Testing* (pp. 159–174). Mahwah, NJ: Lawrence Erlbaum.

Crooks, T. J. (1988, Winter). The impact of classroom evaluation practices on students, *Review of Educational Research, 58(4),* 438–481.

Cross, C. T., & Stempel, A. R. (1995). *Where in the world are we? The need for international benchmarking.* Paper presentation at U.S. Department of Education, Office of Educational Research and Improvement, National Institute on Student Achievement, Curriculum, and Assessment, International benchmarking: Setting world class standards to improve student achievement: Working group meeting. Washington, DC.

DAEU: le diplôme de la seconde chance. (1996, Octobre). *Le Monde de l'Education, 241,* 81–84.

de Marrais, K. B., & Le Compte, M. D. (1999). *The way schools work: A sociological analysis of education, (3rd Ed.).* New York, NY: Addison Wesley Longman.

Debra P. v. Turlington, 644 F.2d 397, 6775 (5th Cir. 1981).

Dempster, F. N. (1991, April). Synthesis of research on reviews and tests, *Educational Leadership,* 71–76.

Dempster, F. N. (1997). Using tests to promote classroom learning. (pp. 332–346). In R. F. Dillon, (Ed.). *Handbook on testing.* Westport, CT: Greenwood Press.

DerSimonian & Laird, (1983). Evaluating the effect of coaching on SAT scores: A meta-analysis, *Harvard Educational Review 53,* 1–5.

Driscoll, L.; Berger, J.B.; Hambleton, R.K.; Keller, L.A.; Maloy, R.W., Hart, D., Oh, P., and Getis, V.; Bowles, S.; Gougeon, F.L.; McDermott, K.A.; Churchill, A. (2003). Education reform: Ten

years after the Massachusetts Education Reform Act of 1993, *Education Connections,* Amherst, MA: University of Massachusetts Amherst School of Education. Retrieved June 16, 2007, from <http://www.thirdeducationgroup.org/Review/Resources/ed.connection.2003.pdf>.

DuBois, P. H. (1964). A test-dominated society: China, 1115 B.C–1905 A.D. In A. Anastasi (Ed.). *Testing problems in perspective: Twenty-fifth anniversary volume of topical readings from the invitational conference on testing problems.* Washington, DC: American Council on Education.

Durham, G. (2000, October 16). Study finds lying, cheating in teens, *Associated Press.*

Eckstein, M. A., & Noah, H. J. (1993). *Secondary school examinations: International perspectives on policies and practice.* New Haven, CT: Yale University Press.

Eckstrom, R. B., Elmore, P. B., & Schafer, W. D. (1997). Standards for educational and psychological test and testing professionals, (pp. 39–64). In R. F. Dillon, (Ed.). *Handbook on testing.* Westport, CT: Greenwood Press.

Edmonds, R. R. & Frederiksen, J. R. (1979). *Search for effective schools: The identification and analysis of city schools that are instructionally effective for poor children.* Washington, D.C.: Educational Resources Information Center.

Education Commission of the States. (2006). *Assessment / High stakes / Competency / Selected Research and Readings.* Retrieved December, 2006 from <http://www.ecs.org/ecsmain.asp?page=/html/issuesK12.asp>.

Engelhart, M. D. & Thomas, M. (1966, Summer). Rice as the inventor of the comparative test, *Journal of Educational Measurement.* 3(2), 141–145.

ETS Board of Trustees, (1991). How can we judge the fairness of tests? *Public Accountability Report,* Princeton, NJ: ETS.

Everding, G. (2006, March 1). Repeated test-taking better for retention than repeated studying, research shows. *Washington University in St. Louis News & Information Service.* Retrieved June 17, 2007 from <http://news-info.wustl.edu/tips/page/normal/6715.html>.

Farkus, S., Johnson, J. & Duffet, A. (1997). *Different drummers : How teachers of teachers view public education.* New York, NY: Public Agenda.

Figlio, D. N., & Lucas, M. E. (2000). Do high grading standards affect student performance? *NBER Working Paper, No. W7985,* National Bureau of Economic Research.

Finneran, K. (Ed.), (2002, October 9). Pioneers in standardized testing. *Issues in Science and Technology, 19(1).* Retrieved May 11, 2007 from <http://www.issues.org/19.1/archives.htm>.

Frary, R. B., Cross, L. H., & Weber, L. J. (1993). Testing and grading practices and opinions of secondary school teachers of academic

subjects: Implications for instruction in measurement, *Educational Measurement: Issues and Practice, 12(3),* 23+.

Freeman, D., et al. (1983). Do textbooks and tests define a national curriculum in elementary school mathematics? *Elementary School Journal, 83(5),* 501–514.

Gandal, M. (1997). Leveraging high-performance with gateway examinations. Paper presented at panel "International Benchmarking: New Findings," at the Annual Meeting of the American Educational Research Association, Chicago, IL.

Gallagher, C. J. (2003). Reconciling a tradition of testing with a new learning paradigm. *Educational Psychology Review. 15(1),* 83–99.

Geisinger, K. F. (2005). The testing industry, ethnic minorities, and individuals with disabilities. In R. P. Phelps (Ed.), *Defending standardized testing* (pp. 187–204). Mahwah, NJ: Lawrence Erlbaum.

GI Forum et al. v. Texas Education Agency et al., F.Supp, 1 (W.D. Tex. 2000)

Goodman, D., & Hambleton, R. K. (2005). Some misconceptions about large-scale educational assessments. In R. P. Phelps, (Ed.), *Defending standardized testing* (pp. 91–110). Mahwah, N.J.: Lawrence Erlbaum.

Gorth, W. P. & Perkins, M. R., Eds., (1979). *A study of minimum competency programs: Final comprehensive report (Volumes 1 & 2).* Amherst, MA: National Evaluation Systems.

Gottfredson, L. S. (2007). Confusion and contention over intelligence testing. In R. P. Phelps, (Ed.), *The Anti-Testing Fallacies.* Washington, DC: American Psychological Association.

Greene, J. P., Winters, M. A., & Forster, G. (2003). *Testing high-stakes tests: Can we believe the results of accountability tests?* Manhattan Institute, Center for Civic Innovation, Report #33.

Greene, J. P., Winters, M. A., & Forster, G. (2004, June). Testing high-stakes tests: Can we believe the results of accountability tests? *Teachers College Record, 106(6),* 1124–1144.

Gullickson, A.R. & Ellwein, M. C. (1985). Post-hoc analysis of teacher-made tests: The goodness of fit between prescription and practice. *Educational Measurement: Issues and Practice, 4(1),* 15–18.

Guskey, T. R. & Gates, S. L. (1986). Synthesis of research on the effects of mastery learning in elementary and secondary classrooms, *Educational Leadership. 43(8),* 73–80.

Haladyna, T. M., Nolen, S. B., & Hass, N. S. (1991, June–July). Raising standardized achievement test scores and the origins of test score pollution. *Educational Researcher,* 20(5), 2–7.

Hambleton, R. K. (2006). Update on MCAS: Is it working? Is it fair? *Third Education Group Review / Essays, 2(7).* Retrieved June 16, 2007, from <http://www.thirdeducationgroup.org/Review/Essays/v2n7.ppt>

Hambleton, R. K, Swaminathan, H., & Rogers, H. J. (1991). *Fundamentals of Item Response Theory.* Newbury Park, CA: SAGE.

Haney, W. M., Madaus, G. F., & Lyons, R. (1993). *The fractured marketplace for standardized testing.* Boston, MA: Kluwer Academic.

Hanushek, E. A., & Raymond, M. E. (2002a, June 9–11). Lessons about the design of state accountability systems. Paper prepared for the conference Taking Account of Accountability: Assessing Policy and Politics, Harvard University.

Hanushek, E. A., & Raymond, M. E. (2002b). Improving educational quality: How best to evaluate our schools? Paper prepared for the conference Education in the 21st Century: Meeting the Challenges of a Changing World, Federal Reserve Bank of Boston, June.

Hanushek, E. A., & Raymond, M. E. (2003). Lessons about the Design of State Accountability Systems. In P. E. Peterson & M. R. West, (Eds.). *No Child Left Behind? The Politics and Practice of Accountability* (pp. 126–151). Washington, D.C.: Brookings Institution.

Hawisher, M. F. & Harper, M. J. (1979). *Competency testing: Bibliography.* Competency Testing Project, Rock Hill, SC: Winthrop College.

Hezlett, S. A., Kuncel, N. R., Vey, M., Ahart, A. M., Ones, D. S., Campbell, J. P., & Camara, W. (2001, April). The effectiveness of the SAT in predicting success early and late in college: A meta-analysis. Paper presented at the annual meeting of the National Council on Measurement in Education, Seattle, WA.

Hills, J. R. (1991). Apathy toward testing and grading. *Phi Delta Kappan* (pp. 540–545), *72.*

Holman, M. G. & Docter, R. F. (1972). *Educational and psychological testing: A study of the industry and its practices.* New York, NY: Russell Sage Foundation.

Houston, C. M. E. (1965). *Joseph Mayer Rice: Pioneer in educational research.* M. S. Thesis, Madison, WI: University of Wisconsin.

Impara, J. C. & Plake, B. S. (1996). Professional development in student assessment for educational administrators. *Educational Measurement: Issues and Practice, 15(2),* 14–20.

International Directory of Company Histories. (2007). Educational Testing Service. Retrieved June 23, 2007 from <http://business.enotes.com/company-histories/educational-testing-service.htm>.

Jackson, M. & Battiste, B. (1978). *Competency testing: An annotated bibliography.* Unpublished manuscript, ERIC: ED167503.

Jacob, B. A. (2001, Fall). Getting tough? *Educational Evaluation and Policy Analysis, 334.*

Jacob, B. A. (2002). Accountability, incentives and behavior: The impact of high-stakes testing in the Chicago Public Schools. *NBER Working Paper No. W8968,* National Bureau of Economic Research, 3.

Jacob, B. A. (2003). High stakes in Chicago. *Education Next, 1.*

Johnson, J. & Immerwahr, J. (1994). *First things first: What Americans expect from the public schools.* New York, NY: Public Agenda.

Kaestle, C. F. (1990, February). The public schools and the public mood. *American Heritage Magazine, 41(1).*

Karpicke, J. D., & Roediger, H. L. (in press). Repeated retrieval during learning is the key to long-term retention. *Journal of Memory and Language.*

Kirkland, M. C. (1971). The effects of tests on students and schools, *Review of Educational Research, 41,* 303–350.

Kobrin, J. L., & Michel, R. (2006). *The SAT as a Predictor of Different Levels of College Performance.* New York, NY: College Board

Koretz, D. M. (1996). Using student assessments for educational accountability, In E.A. Hanushek & D.W. Jorgenson, (Eds.). *Improving America's schools: The role of incentives.* Washington, D.C.: National Academy Press.

Koretz, D. M., Linn, R. L., Dunbar, S. B., & Shepard, L. A. (1991). The effects of high-stakes testing on achievement: Preliminary findings about generalization across tests. Paper presented in R.L. Linn (Chair), Effects of High-Stakes Educational Testing on Instruction and Achievement, symposium presented at the annual meeting of the American Educational Research Association, Chicago, April 5.

Kulik, J. A., Bangert-Drowns, R. L. & Kulik, C-L. C. (1984). Effectiveness of coaching for aptitude tests, *Psychological Bulletin 95,* 179–188.

Kulik, C-L. & Kulik, J. A. (1987). Mastery testing and student learning: A meta-analysis, *Journal of Educational Technology Systems, 15,* 325–345.

Kulik, J. A. & Kulik, C-L. C., (1989). The concept of meta-analysis, *International Journal of Education Research,* 227–340.

Labaree, D. F. (1999, May). The chronic failure of curriculum reform. *Education Week on the Web,* 19.

Leach, M. M. & Oakland, T. (2007). Ethics standards impacting test development and use: A review of 31 ethics codes impacting practices in 35 countries. *International Journal of Testing. 7(1),* 71–88.

Leighton, J. P. (2007). Large-scale cognitive diagnostic testing: Some fallacies. In R. P. Phelps, (Ed.), *The Anti-Testing Fallacies.* Washington, DC: American Psychological Association.

Lincoln, E. A., & Workman, L. L. (1936). *Testing and the uses of test results.* New York, NY: Macmillan.

Linn, R. L. (1993, March). Raising the stakes of test administration: The impact on student performance on NAEP. *CSE Technical Report 360.* Los Angeles, CA: National Center for Research on Evaluation, Standards, and Student Testing, 3.

Linn, R. L. (2000, March). Assessments and accountability. *Educational Researcher,* 4–16.

Linn, R. L., Graue, M. E., & Sanders, N. M. (1990). Comparing state and district results to national norms: The validity of the claims that 'everyone is above average. *Educational Measurement: Issues and Practice, 9(3),* 5–14.

Locke, E. A. & Latham, G. P. (2002, September). Building a practically useful theory of goal setting and task motivation: A 35-year odyssey, *American Psychologist*.

Lohman, D. F. (1997). The history of intelligence testing in context: The impact of personal, religious, and scientific beliefs on the development of theories and tests of human abilities. (pp. 82–106). In R. F. Dillon, (Ed.). *Handbook on testing*. Westport, CT: Greenwood Press.

Lohman, D. F. (2006). Beliefs about differences between ability and accomplishment: From folk theories to cognitive science. *Roeper Review, 29*, 32–40.

Louis, K. S., & Versloot, B. (1996). High standards and cultural diversity: Cautionary tales of comparative research—A comment on "Benchmarking education standards." *Educational Evaluation and Policy Analysis, 18 (3)* 253–61.

Loveless, T. (2003, February 11). Quoted in "New Report Confirms. . ." U.S. Congress: Committee on Education and the Workforce, *Press release*, February 11.

Marsh, E. J., Roediger, H. L., Bjork, R. A. & Bjork, E. L. (in press). The memorial consequences of multiple-choice testing. *Psychonomic Bulletin & Review*.

Mass Insight, (2002, March). *Taking charge*. Boston, MA: Author.

Matthews, J. & Hill, I. (2006). *Supertest: How the International Baccalaureate can strengthen our schools*. Chicago, IL: Open Court

McKenzie, D. E. (1983, April). Research for school improvement: An appraisal of some recent trends. *Educational Researcher, 12(4)*, 5–17.

McKnight, C. C., Crosswhite, F. J., Dossey, J. A., Kifer, E. A., Swafford, J. O., Travers, K. J., & Cooney, T. J. (1987). *The underachieving curriculum: Assessing U.S. school mathematics from an international perspective*. Champaign, IL: Stipes.

McMillan, J. H. (2001, Spring). Secondary teachers' classroom assessment and grading practices. *Educational Measurement: Issues and Practice. 20(1)*.

McRae, D. J. (2006) Comments on 'Lake Woebegone' Twenty Years Later, by J.J. Cannell, M.D. *Third Education Group Review/Essays, 2(2)*. Retrieved June 16, 2007, from <http://www.thirdeducation-group.org/Review/Essays/v2n2.pdf>

Mehrens, W. (1998, July). Consequences of assessment: What is the evidence? *Education Policy Analysis Archives 6 (13)*, 14.

Messick, S. (1984). The psychology of educational measurement. *Journal of Educational Measurement, 21*, 215–237.

Messick, S. & Jungeblut, A. (1981). Time and method in coaching for the SAT, *Psychological Bulletin 89*, 191–216.

Milewski, G. B., & Camara, W. J. (2002, September) *Colleges and universities that do not require SAT or ACT scores*, Office of Research and Development RN-18, New York, NY: College Board.

Milton, O. (1981). *Will that be on the final?* Springfield, IL: Charles C. Thomas Publisher.

Molpus, D. (1998, September 15). Improving high school education, *National Public Radio Morning Edition.*

Monroe, W. S. (1950). *Encyclopedia of educational research,* Rev. Ed. New York, NY: Macmillan.

Mullis, I. V. S. (1997a). Benchmarking toward world-class standards: Some characteristics of the highest performing school systems in the TIMSS. Paper presented at panel "International Benchmarking: New Findings," at the Annual Meeting of the American Educational Research Association, Chicago.

Mullis, I. V. S. (1997b). *Mathematics achievement in the primary school years: IEA's Third International Mathematics and Science Study.* Chestnut Hill, MA: Boston College.

Mullis, I. V. S., M. O. Martin, A. E. Beaton, E. J. Gonzalez, D. L. Kelly, and T. A. Smith. (1998). Mathematics and science achievement in the final year of secondary school: IEA's Third International Mathematics and Science Study. Chestnut Hill, MA: Boston College.

Mund, V. A., & Wolf, R. H. (1971). *Industrial organization and public policy.* New York, NY: Appleton-Century-Crofts.

Murnane, R. J. (1981, Fall). Interpreting the evidence on school effectiveness. *Teachers College Record.* 83(1), 19–35.

National Association of College Admission Counselors (NACAC). (2006, May). *State of college admission 2006.* Alexandria, VA: Author. <http://www.nacacnet.org/NR/rdonlyres/78BCFBFB-6871–4FCA-B1BF-50E330735706/0/06SOCA_ExecutiveSummary pdf.pdf>.

National Association of College Admission Counselors (NACAC). (2006, May). Telephone correspondence.

National Endowment for the Humanities. (1991). *National tests: What other countries expect their students to know.* Washington, DC: Author.

Natriello, G., & Dornbusch, S. M. (1984). *Teacher evaluative standards and student effort.* New York, NY: Longman.

Nave, B., Miech, E. & Mosteller, F. (2000, October). A lapse in standards: Linking standards-based reform with student achievement. *Phi Delta Kappan.*

Needham, D. (1969). *Economic analysis and industrial structure.* New York, NY: Holt, Rinehart & Winston.

New Jersey Department of Education, (1977, November). *Compendium of educational research, planning, evaluation, and assessment activities: USA & Canada.* Division of Research, Planning & Evaluation, Bureau of Research & Assessment, Trenton.

Newbart, D. (2007, June 16). Principal linked to changed grades. *Chicago Sun-Times*

Noble, J. P. (1991). *Predicting college grades from ACT assessment scores and high school course work and grade information,* ACT Research Report 91–3. Iowa City, IA: ACT.

Noble, J. (2004). The effects of using ACT composite scores and high school averages on college admissions decisions for ethnic groups. In R. Zwick (Ed.), *Rethinking the SAT,* (pp. 303–319). New York, NY: RoutledgeFalmer.

Nolan, K. (1997). Implementing world class standards in U.S. state assessment systems. Paper presented at panel, *International Benchmarking: New Findings,* at the Annual Meeting of the American Educational Research Association, Chicago, IL.

Northwest Regional Educational Laboratory. (1990, April). *Effective schooling practices: A research synthesis, 1990 update.* Portland, OR: Author.

O'Boyle, E. & McDaniel, M. A. (2007). Criticisms of employment testing: A commentary. In R. P. Phelps, (Ed.), *The anti-testing fallacies.* Washington, DC: American Psychological Association.

O'Donoghue, J. (2006, June 21). Wilson teacher alleges faulty graduation lists. *Northwest Current* (Washington, DC)

Olson, L. (2002, June 19). Accountability studies find mixed impact on achievement. *Education Week,* 13.

Palmer, J. S. (2002). *Performance incentives, teachers, and students: Estimating the effects of rewards policies on classroom practices and student performance.* Ph.D. dissertation. Columbus, OH: The Ohio State University.

Phelps, R. P. (1994). The fractured marketplace for standardized testing (book review). *Economics of Education Review, 13(4),* 367–370.

Phelps, R. P. (1996, Fall). Are U.S. students the most heavily tested on Earth? *Educational Measurement: Issues and Practice, 15(3),* 19–27.

Phelps, R. P., (1998). The demand for standardized student testing. *Educational Measurement: Issues and Practice, 17(3),* 5–23.

Phelps, R. P. (2000a, Winter). Estimating the cost of systemwide student testing in the United States. *Journal of Education Finance,* 343–380.

Phelps, R. P. (2000b, December). High stakes: Testing for tracking, promotion, and graduation (book review). *Educational and Psychological Measurement, 60(6).*

Phelps, R. P. (2000c). Trends in large-scale, external testing outside the United States. *Educational Measurement: Issues and Practice, 19(1),* 11–21.

Phelps, R. P. (2001, August). Benchmarking to the world's best in Mathematics: Quality control in curriculum and instruction among the top performers in the TIMSS. *Evaluation Review, 25(4),* 391–439.

Phelps, R. P. (2003). *Kill the messenger: The war on standardized testing.* New Brunswick, NJ: Transaction Publishers.

Phelps, R. P., Dietrich, G. L., Phillips, G., & McCormack, K. A. (2003, November). *Higher education: An international perspective.* [ERIC

ED474484, HE035711] Available at <http://www.thirdeducation-group.org/Review/Resources/IntlHigherEducation.htm>.

Phelps, R. P., Ed. (2005a). *Defending standardized testing.* Mahwah, NJ: Lawrence Erlbaum.

Phelps, R. P. (2005b). Persistently positive: Forty years of public opinion on standardized testing. In R. P. Phelps (Ed.), *Defending standardized testing* (pp. 1–22). Mahwah, NJ: Lawrence Erlbaum.

Phelps, R. P. (2005c). Polls and surveys that have included items about standardized testing: 1954 to present. In R. P. Phelps (Ed.), *Defending standardized testing* (pp. 255–280). Mahwah, NJ: Lawrence Erlbaum.

Phelps, R. P. (2005d). The rich, robust research literature on testing's achievement benefits. In R. P. Phelps (Ed.), *Defending standardized testing* (pp. 55–90). Mahwah, NJ: Lawrence Erlbaum.

Phelps, R. P. (2005e). The source of Lake Wobegon. *The Third Education Group Review, 1(2).* http://www.thirdeducationgroup.org/Review/Articles/v1n2.pdf

Phelps, R. P. (2005f). Some studies revealing testing achievement benefits, by methodology type. In R. P. Phelps (Ed.), *Defending standardized testing* (pp. 281–329). Mahwah, NJ: Lawrence Erlbaum.

Phelps, R. P. (2007a, Summer). The dissolution of education knowledge. *Educational Horizons 85(4).*

Phelps, R. P. (2007b). Introduction. In R. P. Phelps, (Ed.), *The anti-testing fallacies.* Washington, DC: American Psychological Association.

Phelps, R. P. (2007c). Educational achievement testing fallacies. In R. P. Phelps, (Ed.), *The anti-testing fallacies.* Washington, DC: American Psychological Association.

Phelps, R. P. (2007d). Summary and conclusion. In R. P. Phelps, (Ed.), *The anti-testing fallacies.* Washington, DC: American Psychological Association.

Phillips, S. E. (1996). Legal defensibility of standards: Issues and policy perspectives. *Educational Measurement: Issues and Practice, 15(2),* 5–13, 19.

Phillips, S. E. (2000). GI Forum v. Texas Education Agency: Psychometric evidence. *Applied Measurement in Education, 13(4).* 343–385.

Plake, B. S. (2005). Doesn't everyone know that 70% is passing? In R. P. Phelps (Ed.). *Defending standardized testing* (pp. 175–186). Mahwah, NJ: Lawrence Erlbaum.

Powell, A. G., Farrar, E. & Cohen, D. K. (1985). *The Shopping Mall High School.* Boston, MA: Houghton Mifflin.

Powers, D. E. (1993). Coaching for the SAT: A summary of the summaries and an update. *Educational Measurement: Issues and Practice.* 24–30, 39.

Powers, D. E., & Rock, D. A. (1999). Effects of coaching on SAT I: Reasoning test scores. *Journal of Educational Measurement, 36 (2),* 93–118.

Powers, D. E., & Kaufman, J. C. (2002). *Do standardized multiple-choice tests penalize deep-thinking or creative students?* (Research Report RR-02–15). Princeton, NJ: Educational Testing Service.

Purkey, S. C. & Smith, M. S. (1983). Effective schools: A review. *The Elementary School Journal. 83(4),* 427–452.

Reichgott, M. (2007, March 26). 'No Child' test demands taxing system. Associated Press.

Resnick, L. B., Nolan, K. J., & Resnick, D. P. (1995). Benchmarking education standards. *Educational Evaluation and Policy Analysis, 17 (4),* 438–61.

Rice, J. M. (1913). *Scientific management in education.* New York, NY: Hinds, Noble & Eldredge.

Roderick, M., Jacob, B. & Bryk, A. (2002). The impact of high-stakes testing in Chicago on student achievement in the promotional gate grades. *Educational Evaluation and Policy Analysis, 24 (4),* 333–57.

Rodgers, G. & Potter, D. L. (1984) *Historical introduction to Leonard P. Ayres' A Measuring Scale for Ability in Spelling (1915)* [Prepared by Donald L. Potter, July 21, 2004, from materials written by Geraldine Rodgers] Retrieved June 18, 2007 from <http://donpotter.net/PDF/Ayres'%20Historical%20Introduction.pdf>.

Roediger, H. L. & Karpicke, J. D. (2006a). The power of testing memory: Basic research and implications for educational practice. *Perspectives on Psychological Science, 1,* 181–210.

Roediger, H.L., & Karpicke, J.D. (2006b). Test-enhanced learning: Taking memory tests improves long-term retention. *Psychological Science, 17,* 249–255.

Roediger, H. L. (2006, December 8). Telephone communication.

Rosswork, S. G. (1977). Goal setting: The effects of an academic task with varying magnitudes of incentive. *Journal of Educational Psychology, 69,* 710–715.

Sawyer, R. L. (1985). *Using demographic information in predicting college freshman grades.* ACT Research Report No. 87, Iowa City, IA: ACT.

Schmidt, F. L. & Hunter, J.E., (1998). The validity and utility of selection methods in Personnel Psychology: Practical and theoretical implication of 85 years of research findings, *Psychological Bulletin, 124,* 262–274.

Schmidt, W. H., Jorde, D., Cogan, L. S., Barrier, E., Gonzalo, I., Moser, U., Shimizu, K., Sawada, T., Valverde, G. A., McKnight, C., Prawat, R. S., Wiley, D., Raizen, S. A., Britton, E. D., & Wolfe, R. G. (1996a). *Characterizing pedagogical flow: An investigation of mathematics and science teaching in six countries.* Boston, MA: Kluwer Academic.

Schmidt, W. H., McKnight, C., Valverde, G. A., Houang, R. T. & Wiley, D. E. (1996b). *Many visions, many aims: A cross-national investiga-*

tion of curricular intentions in school mathematics. Boston, MA: Kluwer Academic.

Schmidt, W. H., McKnight, C. & Raizen, R. A. (1997). *A splintered vision: An investigation of U.S. science and mathematics education.* Boston, MA: Kluwer Academic.

Shanker, A. (1996). A proposal for a national benchmarking institute on educational standards. Washington, DC: American Federation of Teachers.

Shaw, L. (2007, June 24). Set lesson plans stir controversy. *Seattle Times.* Retrieved June 25, 2007 from < http://seattletimes.nwsource. com/>.

Shepard, L. A. (1990). Inflated test score gains: Is the problem old norms or teaching the test? *Educational Measurement: Issues and Practice.* Fall, 15–22.

Shepard, L. A. (2000). The role of assessment in a learning culture. Presidential Address presented at the annual meeting of the American Educational Research Association, New Orleans, LA, April 26.

Sireci, S. G. (2005). The most frequently unasked questions about testing. In R. P. Phelps (Ed.). *Defending standardized testing* (111–122). Mahwah, NJ: Lawrence Erlbaum.

Sireci, S. G. & Hambleton, R. K. (2007). Mission: Protect the public: Licensure and certification testing in the 21st Century. In R. P. Phelps, (Ed.), *The anti-testing fallacies.* Washington, DC: American Psychological Association.

Smyth, F. L. (1990). SAT coaching: What really happens to scores and how we are led to expect more. *The Journal of College Admissions,* 129, 7–16.

Snedecor, P. J. (1989). Coaching: Does it pay—revisited. *Journal of College Admissions, 125,* 15–18.

Southern Regional Education Board. (1998). *High Schools That Work: Case studies.* Available at <www.sreb.org>.

Staats, A. (1973). Behavior analysis and token reinforcement in educational behavior modification and curriculum research, In C. E. Thoreson, (Ed.), *72nd Yearbook of the NSSE, Behavior modification in education.* Chicago, IL: University of Chicago Press.

Starch, D., & Elliot, E. C. (1912). Reliability of the grading of high school work in English. *School Review, 21,* 442–457.

Starch, D., & Elliot, E. C. (1913a). Reliability of the grading of high school work in history. *School Review, 21,* 676–681.

Starch, D., & Elliot, E. C. (1913b). Reliability of grading work in mathematics. *School Review, 22,* 254–259.

Stevenson, H. W., & Stigler, J. W. (1992). *The learning gap: Why our schools are failing and what we can learn from Japanese and Chinese education.* New York, NY: Summit.

Stevenson, H. W. & Lee, S-Y., et al. (1997). *International comparisons of entrance and exit examinations: Japan, United Kingdom, France,*

and Germany. Washington, DC: U.S. Department of Education, Office of Educational Research and Improvement.

Stiggins, R. J., Frisbee, D. A. & Griswold, P. A. (1989). Inside high school grading practices: Building a research agenda. *Educational Measurement: Issues and Practice.* 8(2), 5–14.

Stiggins, R. J., & Conklin, N. F. (1992). *In teachers' hands: Investigating the practices of classroom assessment.* New York, NY: SUNY Press.

Stone, J. E. (1995). Inflated grades, inflated enrollment, and inflated budgets: An analysis and call for review at the state level. *Education Policy Analysis Archives, 3(11).*

Stone, J. E. (2002, May). Value-added achievement gains of NBPTS-certified teachers in Tennessee: A brief report, *Briefings in Educational Research, 2(5),* Retrieved June 23, 2007 from <http://www.education-consumers.com/oldsite/briefs/stoneNBPTS.shtm>.

Strauss, V. (2006, October 10). The rise of the testing culture. *Washington Post,* A09.

Stricherz, M. (2001, May 9). Many teachers ignore cheating, survey finds. *Education Week on the Web.*

Stricker, L. J., Rock, D. A., Burton, N. W., Muraki, E., & Jirele, T. J. (1994). Adjusting college grade point average criteria for variations in grading standards: A comparison of methods. *Journal of Applied Psychology, 79 (2),* 178–183.

Tinkelman, S. N. (1965, October 30). Regents examinations in New York State after 100 years, In R. L. Ebel (Ed.), *Invitational conference on testing problems,* New York City, Princeton, NJ: Educational Testing Service.

Toch, T. (2007). *Margins of error.* Washington, DC: Education Sector.

Tuckman, B. W. (1994, April 4–8). *Comparing incentive motivation to metacognitive strategy in its effect on achievement.* Paper presented at the Annual Meeting of the American Educational Research Association, New Orleans, LA, Available from ERIC (ED368790).

Tuckman, B. W., & Trimble, S. (1997, August). *Using tests as a performance incentive to motivate eighth-graders to study.* Paper presented at the Annual Meeting of the American Psychological Association, Chicago, IL, Available from ERIC (ED418785).

Tyack, D. B. (1974). *The one best system: A history of American education.* Cambridge, MA: Harvard University Press.

USA Today. (2001, August 30). High schools inflate grades, and parents are fooled, 12a.

U.S. Department of Education, Office of Educational Research and Improvement, National Institute on Student Achievement, Curriculum, and Assessment. (1995). International benchmarking: Setting world class standards to improve student achievement. Working group meeting, Washington, DC.

U.S. Department of Education, Office of Educational Research and Improvement. (1996). *Pursuing excellence: A study of U.S. eighth-*

grade mathematics and science teaching, learning, curriculum, and achievement in international context (NCES 97–198). Washington, DC: U.S. Department of Education.

U.S. General Accounting Office. (1993a). *Educational testing: The Canadian experience with standards, examinations, and assessments,* (GAO/PEMD-93–11). Washington, DC: Author.

Whitla, D.K. (1988). Coaching: Does it pay? Not for Harvard students. *The College Board Review. 148,* 32–35.

Wildemuth, B. M. (1977). *Minimal competency testing: Issues and procedures, an annotated bibliography.* ERIC ED150188.

Woodruff, D. J., & Ziomek, R. L. (2004a, March). *Differential grading standards among high schools.* ACT Research Report 2004–2, Iowa City, IA: ACT.

Woodruff, D. J., & Ziomek, R. L. (2004b, March). *High School Grade Inflation from 1991 to 2003.* ACT Research Report 2004–4, Iowa City, IA: ACT.

Wyatt, E. (2001, August 23). Schools found uneven in promotion of students, *The New York Times.*

Yazzie-Mintz, E. (2007, June 1). *Voices of students on engagement: A report on the 2006 High School Survey of Student Engagement.* Bloomington, IN: Center for Evaluation & Education Policy, Indiana University School of Education.

Zehr, M. A. (2001, April 4). Study: Test-preparation courses raise scores only slightly. *Education Week.*

Zeng, K. (1999). *Dragon gate: Competitive examinations and their consequences.* London: Cassell.

Ziomek, R. L., & Andrews, K. M. (1996). *Predicting the college grade point averages of special-tested students from their ACT assessment scores and high school grades.* ACT Research Report 96–7. Iowa City, IA: ACT.

Zwick, R. (2007). College admission testing. Washington, DC: NACAC. Retrieved June 21, 2007 from <http://www.nacacnet.org/NR/rdonlyres/26606B59-5725-4A4B-9203-8D12D805B7C8/0/FinalStandardizedTestingWhitePaper.pdf>

Nonprint resources & journals [proprietary products] (purpose or activities)

Achieve (policy research and analysis and standards benchmarking services)

> 8 Story Street, First Floor
> Cambridge, MA 02138
> 617.496.6300
> 400 N. Capitol Street, NW
> Suite 351
> Washington, DC 20001
> 202.624.1460

talk-to-us@achieve.org
http://www.achieve.org

ACT, Inc. [ACT, PLAN, EXPLORE, COMPASS, ASSET, WorkKeys, CAAP]
ACT National Office
2201 North Dodge Street
P.O. Box 168
Iowa City, IA 52243-0168
319.337.1000
http://www.act.org/

ACT Research (research and analysis)
http://www.act.org/research

American Federation of Teachers (member association)
555 New Jersey Ave. N.W.,
Washington, DC 20001
202.879.4400
http://www.aft.org/

American National Standards Institute (ANSI) (U.S. member of International Standards Organization)
1819 L Street, NW, 6th floor
Washington, DC 20036
202.293.8020
info@ansi.org
http://www.ansi.org/

American Psychological Association (APA) (member association)
750 First Street, NE
Washington, DC 20002-4242
800.374.2721 or 202.336.5500
http://www.apa.org/science/testing.html
PsycINFO
http://www.apa.org/psycinfo/about

Division 5: Evaluation, Measurement, and Statistics
http://www.apa.org/about/division/div5.html

Applied Measurement in Education (scholarly journal)
http://www.tandf.co.uk/journals/titles/08957347.asp

Applied Measurement Professionals (AMP) (develop certification and licensure tests)
18000 W. 105th Street
Olathe, KS 66061.7543 USA
913.895.4600
INFO-AMP@goamp.com
http://www.goamp.com/Default.htm

Assessment Systems Corporation (develops data analysis software for tests)
2233 University Ave.

Suite 200
St. Paul, MN 55114
651.64 7.9220
http://www.assess.com/

Association of American Medical Colleges (AAMC) [MCAT]
2450 N St. NW
Washington, DC 20037-1127
mcat@aamc.org
http://www.aamc.org/

Association of American Publishers: School Division (trade
association)
50 F Street, N.W.
Washington, D.C. 20001
202.347.3375
jdiskey@publishers.org
http://www.publishers.org/home/abouta/test.htm/

Association of Test Publishers (ATP) (trade association)
1201 Pennsylvania Avenue, N.W.
Suite 300
Washington D.C. 20004
866.240.7909
http://www.testpublishers.org/

Armed Services Vocational Aptitude Battery (ASVAB)
ASVAB Career Development Program
http://www.asvabprogram.com/

Battelle for Kids (support for value-added assessment programs)
41 South High Street, Suite 2240
Columbus, Ohio 43215
614.469.5966
http://www.battelleforkids.com/b4k/rt/about

Bridges/TestU (assessment software)
33637-B Hwy 97 N.
Oroville, WA 98844
250.869.4200
http://www.bridges.com/us/prodnserv/index.html

Buros Institute of Mental Measurements [*Mental Measurements
Yearbook*] (testing research and analysis)
bimm@unl.edu
Buros Institute for Assessment Consultation and Outreach
(test development consulting services)
biaco@unl.edu bi
University of Nebraska
21 Teachers College Hall
Lincoln, NE 68588-0348
402.472.6203
http://www.unl.edu/buros

California Department of Education, Policy and Evaluation
Division [APR, STAR, CAHSEE]
Academic Performance Index Research Reports
1430 N Street
Sacramento, CA 95814
916.319.0863
http://www.cde.ca.gov/ta/ac/ar/index.asp

Caveon Test Security (test security advisory services)
12227 S. Business Park Dr.
Suite 120
Draper, Utah 84020
http://www.caveon.com/

Center for Academic Integrity (research on ethics and behavior)
Box 90434
Duke University
Durham, North Carolina 27708
919.660.3045
integrity@duke.edu
http://www.academicintegrity.org/index.asp

Center for Applied Linguistics (language test development and
translation services)
4646 40th Street NW
Washington DC 20016-1859
202.362.0700
info@cal.org
http://www.cal.org/about/index.html

Center for Educational Assessment (CEA) (test development
services)
Research and Evaluation Methods Program (REMP)
(research and analysis of tests)
School of Education
152 Hills South
University of Massachusetts
Amherst, MA 01003
413.545.0262
http://www.umass.edu/education/cea/main.htm

Center for Educational Research and Evaluation (test development
analysis and services)
Department of Educational Research Methodology
School of Education
University of North Carolina – Greensboro
211 Curry Building, P.O. Box 26170
Spring Garden Street,
Greensboro, NC 27402-6170
336.334.5882

rahill@uncg.edu
http://www.uncg.edu/erm/ermCERE.html

Center for Educational Testing and Evaluation (CETE) [Kansas
Assessments]
University of Kansas
1122 West Campus Road
735 Joseph R. Pearson Hall
Lawrence, KS 66045
785.864.3537
cete@ku.edu
http://www.cete.ku.edu/

Cito [Dutch national examinations, school examinations]
P.O. Box 1034
6801 MG Arnhem
The Netherlands
+31 26 352 11 11
http://www.cito.nl/com_index.htm

CollegeBoard [SAT, Advanced Placement exams]
45 Columbus Avenue
New York, NY 10023-6992
212.713.8000
http://www.collegeboard.org/

Council of Chief State School Officers (CCSSO) [State Student
Assessment Programs Database]
One Massachusetts Ave., NW
Suite 700
Washington, DC 20001-1431
info@ccsso.org
http://www.ccsso.org/

Council on Licensure, Enforcement and Regulation (CLEAR)
(member association)
403 Marquis Avenue
Suite 200
Lexington, KY 40502
859.269.1289
http://www.clearhq.org/

Council of the Great City Schools (association of large-city school
districts)
1301 Pennsylvania Avenue, NW
Suite 702
Washington, DC 20004
202.393.2427
http://www.cgcs.org

Council of Ministers of Education of Canada (CMEC) (pan-
Canadian cooperative group)
CMEC Secretariat

95 St. Clair Avenue West, Suite 1106
Toronto, Ontario   M4V 1N6
Canada
416.962.8100
information@cmec.ca
http://www.cmec.ca/abouteng.stm

CTB McGraw/Hill Assessment Products and Services [TerraNova,
CTBS, CAT, Acuity, Test of Cognitive Skills, InView]
20 Ryan Ranch Road
Monterey, CA 93940
800.538.9547
http://www.ctb.com

Data Recognition Corporation (DRC) (custom large-scale test
development and survey services)
13490 Bass Lake Road
Maple Grove, MN 55311
800.826.2368
mail@datarecognitioncorp.com
www.datarecognitioncorp.com

Defense Activity for Non-Traditional Education Support (DANTES)
(test administration service for military personnel (for non-
military tests))
6490 Saufley Field Road
Pensacola, FL 32509-5243
850.452.1111
dantes@voled.doded.mil
http://www.dantes.doded.mil/dantes_web/danteshome.
asp?Flag=True

Dyslexia Action (U.K.) (assessment research and consulting related
to reading)
Park House, Wick Road
Egham
Surrey TW20 0HH
01784.222300
info@dyslexiaaction.org.uk
http://www.dyslexiaaction.org.uk/

Educational Horizons (scholarly journal)
http://www.pilambda.org/

Educational and Industrial Testing Service (EdITS)
[IRIS, COPS Interest Inventory, MAACL-R, DOSC]
P.O. Box 7234
San Diego, CA 92167
customerservice@edits.net
800.416.1666
http://www.edits.net/

Educational and Psychological Measurement (scholarly journal)
http://epm.sagepub.com/

Educational Records Bureau [CTP, ISEE, WrAP]
220 East 42nd Street, Suite 100
New York, NY 10017
212.672.9800
http://www.erbtest.org

Educational Research Information Center (ERIC) (database of
education research articles, papers, and statistical
compendia)
http://eric.ed.gov/
http://ericae.net/

Educational Testing Service (ETS) [GRE, Praxis, PSAT, TOEFL, TESL,
IAEP, CLEP]
Rosedale Road
Princeton, NJ 08541
http://www.ets.org

Educators' Computer Software [TestLynx]
411 Western Lane
Irmo, SC 29063
800.688.3551
http://www.testchamp.com/AboutUs.html

ERIC Test Locator (searchable database of tests)
http://buros.unl.edu/buros/jsp/search.jsp

ETS Research (research and analysis)
http://www.ets.org/portal/site/ets/menuitem.22f30af61d3
4e9c39a77b13bc3921509/?vgnextoid=73b2be3a864f4010V
gnVCM10000022f95190RCRD

ETS Test Link (searchable database of tests)
http://www.ets.org/testcoll/index.html

European Test Publishers Group (trade association)
c/o OnlyConnectLtd.
+44.1491.573648
+44.1491.573648
ian.florance@btinternet.com
http://www.etpg.org/

Fisher Education Consulting, LLC (test development services)
555 Hickory Blvd.
McMinnville, TN 37110
931.668.0775
http://www.fishereducation.com

Gallup Organization (custom survey and test development)
1001 Gallup Drive
Omaha, NE 68102

412.951.2003
http://www.gallup.com/

General Educational Development Testing Service [GED]
American Council on Education,
Center for Adult Learning & Education Credentials
(CALEC)
One Dupont Circle NW, Suite 250
Washington DC, 20036
202.939.9475
http://www.acenet.edu/calec/ged

Graduate Management Admission Council (GMAC) [GMAT]
1600 Tysons Blvd., Ste. 1400
McLean, VA 22102
703.749.0131
webmaster@gmac.com
http://www.gmac.com

Harcourt Educational Measurement / Psychological Corporation
[Stanford, Metropolitan, Differential Aptitude Test (DAT),
Otis-Lennon, Miller Analogies, TAP, Wechsler]
19500 Bulverde Road
San Antonio, Texas 78259
800.872.1726
http://www.psychcorp.com

The Industrial-Organizational Psychologist (scholarly journal)
http://www.siop.org/tip/TIP.aspx

Insite (test development, training, data collection)
2700 Middleburg Drive, Suite 220
Columbia, SC 29204
803.933.9690
http://insitesc.com

Institute for Objective Measurement, Inc. (member organization of
Rasch Modelers)
155 North Harbor Drive, Suite 1002
Chicago, IL 60601
312.616.6705
InstObjMeas@Worldnet.att.net
http://www.rasch.org/index.htm

Intelligence (scholarly journal)
http://www.elsevier.com/wps/find/journaldescription.cws_
home/620195/description#description

International Association for the Evaluation of Educational
Achievement (IEA) [FIMSS, SIMSS, TIMSS, IRLS, PIRLS,
CivED, TIMSS-R, ICCS]
Herengracht 487
1017 BT

Amsterdam
The Netherlands
http://www.iea.nl/

International Baccalaureate (operates combined curriculum and
testing program, used worldwide)
IB Headquarters
Route des Morillons 15
Grand-Saconnex, Genève
CH-1218
SWITZERLAND
+41.22.791.7740
ibhq@ibo.org
http://www.ibo.org/

IB Curriculum and Assessment Center
Peterson House, Malthouse Avenue
Cardiff Gate
Cardiff, Wales
CF23 8GL
UNITED KINGDOM
+44.29.2054.7777
ibca@ibo.org

International Indicators of Education Systems (INES) Project.
Organisation for Economic Co-operation and
Development (OECD)
Network A: Learning Outcomes
http://nces.ed.gov/surveys/international/ines/index.
asp?INESSection=A

International Personnel Management Association and Assessment
Council (trade association)
c/o IPMA-HR
1617 Duke Street
Alexandria, VA 22314
703.549.7100
http://www.ipmaac.org/

International Standards Organization (ISO) (develops international
standards)
ISO Central Secrétariat
1, ch. de la Voie-Creuse
Case Postale 56
CH-1211 Geneva 20
Switzerland
+41.22.749.01.11
central@iso.org
www.iso.org

International Test Commission (ITC) (develops international testing standards)
http://www.intestcom.org/

Internet Resources for Higher Education Outcomes Assessment (list of resources)
University Planning and Analysis
North Carolina State University
http://www2.acs.ncsu.edu/UPA/assmt/resource.htm

Iowa Testing Programs [ITBS, ITED]
N459 Lindquist Center
University of Iowa School of Education
Iowa City, IA 52242-1529
319.335.5408
educationiowa@uiowa.edu
http://www.education.uiowa.edu/itp/itbs/

Journal of Applied Testing Technology (online journal)
http://www.testpublishers.org/atp_journal.htm

Law School Admission Council [LSAT]
P.O. Box 40
Newtown, PA 18940
215.968.1001
http://www.lsac.org

Let's Talk About Testing Web site (answers to individual questions)
http://www.ets.org/testing/

Maryland Assessment Research Center for Education Success (MARCES)
Department of Measurement, Statistics, and Evaluation
College of Education
University of Maryland
College Park, MD 20742-1115
301.405.3620
http://www.marces.org/

Mass Insight Education (education analysis and advocacy in Massachusetts)
18 Tremont Street, Suite 930
Boston, MA 02108
617.722.4160
http://www.massinsight.org/

Measured Progress [Progress Toward Standards (PTS), ProFile]
171 Watson Road
P.O. Box 1217
Dover, NH 03820
603.749.9102
http://www.measuredprogress.org/

Measurement Incorporated (test scoring services)
423 Morris Street
Durham, NC 27701
919.683.2413
http://www.measinc.com/

MetaMetrics (consulting and analysis linking instruction to
assessments)
1000 Park Forty Plaza Drive, Suite 120
Durham, North Carolina 27713
919.547.3400
webinfo@Lexile.com
webinfo@Quantiles.com
http://www.metametricsinc.com/

Mid-Atlantic Psychometric Services, Inc. (test development
services)
212 Ashton Dr., SW
Leesburg, VA 20175-2527

MindPlay (assessment software)
440 S. Williams Blvd., Suite #206
Tucson, AZ 85711-4403
800.221.7911
mail@mindplay.com
800.221.7911
http://www.mindplay.com/

National Assessment Governing Board (bipartisan commission that
oversees the NAEP)
800 North Capitol Street, N.W, Suite 825
Washington, D.C. 20002
202.357.6938
http://www.nagb.org/

National Association for College Admission Counseling (NACAC)
1631 Prince Street
Alexandria, Virginia 22314
703.836-2222
info@nacac.com
http://www.nacacnet.org/MemberPortal/
ProfessionalResources/Research/Testing.htm

Standardized Testing Bibliography
http://www.nacacnet.org/NR/rdonlyres/B16EAF26-3362-
405F-A2B0-8CCD9A2A3EDD/0/Testing_Bibl.pdf/

National Association of School Psychologists (member association)
4340 East West Highway
Suite 402
Bethesda, MD 20814
301.657.0270

center@naspweb.org
http://www.nasponline.org/

National Association of Test Directors (NATD) (member association)
http://www.natd.org/

National Board of Medical Examiners [USMLE]
3750 Market Street
Philadelphia, PA 19104-3102
215.590.9500
webmail@nbme.org
http://www.nbme.org/

National Center for Developmental Education (postsecondary
developmental (i.e., remedial) testing research and
analysis)
Reich College of Education
Appalachian State University
Boone, North Carolina 28608
828.262.3057
http://www.ncde.appstate.edu/

National Center for Educational Accountability/Just for the Kids
(data analysis services)
4030-2 West Braker Lane
Austin, Texas 78759
800.762.4645
jftk@just4kids.org
http://www.just4kids.org/en/

National Center for Educational Outcomes (NCEO) (special
education testing research, analysis)
University of Minnesota
350 Elliott Hall
75 East River Road
Minneapolis, MN 55455
612.626.1530
http://education.umn.edu/NCEO/

National Center for Education Statistics (NCES) (reports results of
NAEP)
U.S. Department of Education
1990 K Street, N.W.
Washington, D.C. 20006
202.502.7300
http://nces.ed.gov/

National Council for Measurement in Education (NCME) (member
association)
2810 Crossroads Drive, Suite 3800
Madison WI, 53718
608.443.2487
http://www.ncme.org/

National Evaluation Systems (NES) (develops state teacher
     certification tests)
     P.O. Box 226
     Amherst, MA 01004-0226
     413.256.0444
     http://www.nesinc.com/mainpage.htm

National Governors' Association Center for Best Practices (policy
     research and analysis)
     Center for Best Practices
     Hall of States
     444 N. Capitol St.
     Washington, D.C. 20001-1512
     202.624.5300
     http://www.nga.org

National Merit Scholarship Corporation (administers university
     scholarship programs)
     1560 Sherman Avenue
     Suite 200
     Evanston, Illinois 60201-4897
     847.866.5100
     http://www.nationalmerit.org/

National Organization for Competency Assurance (NOCA) (trade
     association)
     2025 M Street, N.W.
     Suite 800
     Washington, DC 20036
     202.367.1165
     http://www.noca.org/

National Survey of Student Engagement (research on measuring
     postsecondary outcomes)
     Center for Postsecondary Research
     Indiana University
     1900 E. Tenth St.
     Eigenmann Hall Suite 419
     Bloomington, IN 47406-7512
     812.856.5150
     nsse@indiana.edu
     http://nsse.iub.edu/html/staff.cfm

National Writing Board [National History Exam] (college
     admissions program)
     730 Boston Post Road, Suite 24
     Sudbury, MA 01776
     800.331.5007
     http://www.tcr.org/

New York State Office of State Assessment [State Assessments,
     Regents Exams, Regents Competency Exams]

University of the State of New York
New York State Education Department
Office of State Assessment
89 Washington Avenue
Albany, New York 12234
518.486.5765
emscassessinfo@mail.nysed.gov
http://www.nysedregents.org/testing/hsregents.html

Northwest Evaluation Association [Measures of Academic Progress
(MAP), Achievement Level Tests, Learning Continuum]
12909 SW 68th Parkway, Suite 400
Portland, Oregon 97223
503.624.1951
http://www.nwea.org/

Numerical Algorithms Group (NAG) (mathematical analysis
software)
1431 Opus Place
Suite 220
Downers Grove, IL 60515-1362
630.971.2337
infodesk@nag.com
http://www.nag.com/

Operation Public Education (research and consulting on value-
added testing)
Center for Greater Philadelphia
3701 Chestnut Street, 6th Fl. East
Philadelphia, PA 19104
215.898.8713
cgpinfo@pobox.upenn.edu
http://www.cgp.upenn.edu/ope.html

Organisation for Economic Co-operation and Development (OECD)
[PISA]
Programme for International Student Assessment (PISA)
Statistics and Indicators Division
2 rue Andre-Pascal
75775 Paris
CEDEX 16, France
http://www.pisa.oecd.org/index.htm/

Pacific Metrics Corporation (test development services)
585 Cannery Row, Suite 201
Monterey, California 93940
831.333.1620
info@pacificmetrics.com
http://www.pacificmetrics.com

Pearson Educational Measurement (large-scale test development,
administration, and scoring)

2510 N. Dodge Street
Iowa City, IA 52245
319.339.6793
5601 Green Valley Drive
Bloomington, Minnesota 55437
800.431.1421
http://www.pearson.com/

Performance Assessment Network (PAN) (develops Web-based tests, POET, Vita)
11590 N. Meridian, Suite 200
Carmel, IN 46032
877.449.8378
info@pantesting.com
http://www.panpowered.com

Performance Indicators in Primary Schools (PIPS) Project (value-added testing consortium)
Curriculum, Evaluation, and Management Project
University of Durham, UK
http://www.pipsproject.org/

Practical Assessment, Research, and Evaluation (online journal)
http://pareonline.net/Home.htm

PRO-ED, Inc. (test critiques, database management, publishing)
8700 Shoal Creek Boulevard
Austin, Texas 78757-6897
800.897.3202
http://www.proedinc.com/

Psychological Assessment Resources (develops diagnostic tests)
16204 North Florida Avenue
Lutz, FL 33549
800.331.8378
http://www3.parinc.com/

Psychometric Society (member association)
University of North Carolina-Greensboro
210 Curry Building
P.O. Box 26171
Greensboro, NC 27402-6171
http://www.psychometricsociety.org/

Questar Assessment [Degrees of Reading Power, TASA Literacy, Core Knowledge Tests]
Hardscrabble Heights, PO Box 382
Brewster, NY 10509-0382
845.277.8100 Fax: 845.277.8115
http://www.tasa.com/

Renaissance Learning [STAR, Accelerated Reader, Math]
PO Box 8036

Wisconsin Rapids, Wisconsin 54495-8036
800.656.6740
answers@renlearn.com
http://www.renlearn.com/aboutus.htm

Riverdeep [Destination Success, Skill Detective, Skill Navigator]
100 Pine Street, Suite 1900
San Francisco, CA 94111
415.659.2000
info@riverdeep.net

222 3rd Ave SE, 4th Floor
Cedar Rapids, IA 52401
319.395.9626
http://www.riverdeep.net/portal/page?_
pageid=353,110771&_dad=portal&_schema= PORTAL

Riverside Publishing [Iowa Tests, CAT, Stanford-Binet, Gates-
MacGinitie, Woodcock-Johnson, Nelson-Denny, NJPASS]
425 Spring Lake Drive
Itasca, IL 60143-2079
800.323.9540
http://www.riverpub.com/

SAS in School Assessment Services, SAS Institute (value-added
testing services)
SAS in School
SAS Campus Drive, Building U
Cary, NC 27513
919.531.7505
http://www.sasinschool.com/

Scantron (assessment data capture and processing)
34 Parker
Irvine California, 92618-1604
800.722.6876
customer_service@scantron.com
http://www.scantron.com/

Scholastic Testing Service (early grades readiness and independent
high school admissions)
4320 Green Ash Drive
Earth City, MO 63045
314.739.3650
ststesting@email.com
http://www.ststesting.com/

Scientific Software International (SSI) (test analysis software)
7383 N. Lincoln Avenue, Suite 100
Lincolnwood, IL 60712-1747 USA
847.675.0720
irt@ssicentral.com
http://www.ssicentral.com/

Second Language Testing, Inc. (test development & translation services)
6135 Executive Blvd
Rockville MD 20852
301.231.6046
CStansfield@2LTI.com
http://www.2lti.com/home2.htm

Slosson Educational Publications, Inc. (special education test development)
P.O. Box 280
East Aurora, NY 14052
888.SLOSSON
slosson@slosson.com
http://www.slosson.com/

Society of Industrial-Organizational Psychologists (SIOP) (member association)
Division 14 of the American Psychological Association
P.O. Box 87
520 Ordway Ave.
Bowling Green, OH 43402-0087
419.353.0032
http://www.siop.org/

Society for Personality Assessment (SPA) (member association)
6109H Arlington Blvd.
Falls Church, VA 22044
703.534.4772
manager@SPAonline.org
http://www.personality.org/

Sociology of Education Research Group (SERG) (policy research and analysis)
Department of Sociology
The University of Houston
491 Philip G. Hoffman Hall
Houston, TX 77204-3012
713.743.3953
GDworkin@uh.edu
http://www.sociology.uh.edu/

Southern Regional Education Board (SREB) (state members association)
592 10th St. N.W.
Atlanta, GA 30318
404.875.9211
http://www.sreb.org/

Standard & Poors, School Evaluation Services (data analysis, statistical indicator development)
55 Water Street

New York, NY 10041

212.438.7984

http://www.standardandpoors.com/ProductsAndServices/
CreditMarketServices/SchoolEvaluationServices/School.
html

Statistics Canada [International Adult Literacy and Life Skills
Survey (IALS)]
150 Tunney's Pasture Driveway
Ottawa, Ontario
K1A 0T6
800.263.1136
infostats@statcan.ca
http://www.statcan.ca/english/about/abtstc.htm

Stoelting Company (physiology research instruments, psychological
& special education tests)
20 Wheat Lane
Wood Dale, IL 60191
630.860.9700
info@stoeltingco.com
http://www.stoeltingco.com/

Système Méthologique d'Aide a la Réalisation de Tests (SMART)
[TIMI, e-NGELS, CGQTS]
Université de Liège
Traverse des Architectes 4,
B3c
B-4000 Liège
Belgium
+32.0.4.366.20.78
smart@ulg.ac.be
http://www.smart.ulg.ac.be/index.php3

Talent Assessment, Inc. (vocational education assessment services
and training)
P.O. Box 508
Jacksonville, FL 32247
800.634.1472
talenta@bellsouth.net

Teaching Research Institute (developers of teacher work sample
methodology)
School of Education
Western Oregon University
345 North Monmouth Ave.
Monmouth, OR 97361
503.838.8391
http://www.tr.wou.edu

TestingFACTS.org (information and resources for understanding
educational testing)

Association of American Publishers – School Division
50 F Street, NW, 4th Floor
Washington, DC 20001
202.347.3375
jdiskey@publishers.org
TestingFACTS.org

Third Education Group (policy research and analysis)
mail@thirdeducationgroup.org
http://www.thirdeducationgroup.org/

Third Education Group Review (online journal)
http://www.thirdeducationgroup.org/Review/TEGreview.
htm

Thompson Prometric (operates computer-based testing centers)
800.370.4169
http://www.prometric.com/

South-Western Learning [ExamView]
800-354-9706
http://www.swlearning.com/examview/examview_main.
html

TIMSS & PIRLS International Study Center
(data management and analysis for TIMSS & PIRLS multi-
country assessments)
Manresa House
140 Commonwealth Ave.
Chestnut Hill, MA 02467
617.552.1600
isc@bc.edu
http://timss.bc.edu/

U.S. Department of Defense
Defense Manpower Data Center
Personnel Testing Program
99 Pacific St., Suite 155A
Monterey, CA 93940-2453
408.655.0400

U.S. Department of Labor
Employment and Training Administration
Frances Perkins Building
200 Constitution Avenue, NW
Washington, DC 20210
877.872.5627
http://www.doleta.gov/etainfo/

U.S. Department of State [Foreign Service Officer Test, Oral
Assessments]
HR/REE/REC
2401 E Street NW

Suite 518 H
Washington, DC 20522
http://careers.state.gov/FS.html

U.S. National Research Center for the Third International
Mathematics & Science Study (TIMSS)
455 Erickson Hall
College of Education
Michigan State University
East Lansing, MI 48824-1034
517.353.775
http://ustimss.msu.edu/middle.htm

Vantage Learning [SPMS, UOTS, Itellimetric, WebCCAT]
110 Terry Drive, Suite 100
Newtown, PA 18940
800.230.2213
http://www.vantagelearning.com/school/

VocationalPsychology.com (links and contact information: test
publishers)
http://www.vocationalpsychology.com/publish.htm

Westat (administration and sample design for large-scale tests,
including the NAEP, PISA, and IEA exams)
1650 Research Blvd.
Rockville, MD 20850
301.251.1500
http://www.westat.com/

WestEd (test development and analysis services)
730 Harrison Street
San Francisco, California 94107
415.615.3219
mkerr@wested.org
http://www.wested.org/cs/we/print/docs/we/home.htm

Western Psychological Services (develops diagnostic tests)
12031 Wilshire Blvd.
Los Angeles, CA 90025-1251
800.648.8857
customerservice@wpspublish.com
http://portal.wpspublish.com/portal/page?_pageid=
53,53086&_dad=portal&_schema=PORTAL

Wonderlic (develops employment tests)
1795 N. Butterfield Rd.
Suite 200
Libertyville, IL 60048
800.323.3742
info@wonderlic.com
http://www.wonderlic.com/

Wrightslaw (advice and advocacy on special education law)
webmaster@wrightslaw.com
http://www.wrightslaw.com/

Peter Lang PRIMERS
in Education

Peter Lang Primers are designed to provide a brief and concise introduction or supplement to specific topics in education. Although sophisticated in content, these primers are written in an accessible style, making them perfect for undergraduate and graduate classroom use. Each volume includes a glossary of key terms and a References and Resources section.

Other published and forthcoming volumes cover such topics as:

- Standards
- Popular Culture
- Critical Pedagogy
- Literacy
- Higher Education
- John Dewey
- Feminist Theory and Education

- Studying Urban Youth Culture
- Multiculturalism through Postformalism
- Creative Problem Solving
- Teaching the Holocaust
- Piaget and Education
- Deleuze and Education
- Foucault and Education

Look for more Peter Lang Primers to be published soon. To order other volumes, please contact our Customer Service Department:

800-770-LANG (within the US)
212-647-7706 (outside the US)
212-647-7707 (fax)

To find out more about this and other Peter Lang book series, or to browse a full list of education titles, please visit our website:

www.peterlang.com